it's all about **change**

T0126339

OSHO

it's all about **change**

the greatest challenge to create a
golden future for humanity

THE WORLD CRISIS – A CRISIS OF CONSCIOUSNESS

OSHO

This is an updated and expanded edition of *The Greatest Challenge –The Golden
Future*

This book was compiled and edited as a special edition on a request by Osho.
The material in this book is selected from various talks by Osho. All of Osho's
talks have been published in full as books, and all talks are available as original
audio recordings. The audio recordings and the complete text archive can be
found via the online OSHO Library at www.osho.com/Library

OSHO MEDIA INTERNATIONAL
New York • Zurich • Mumbai
an imprint of
OSHO INTERNATIONAL
www.osho.com/oshointernational

Distributed by Publishers Group Worldwide
www.pgw.com

Library of Congress Catalog-In-Publication Data is available

Printed in India by Manipal Technologies Limited, Karnataka

Print edition: ISBN-13: 978-1-938755-93-4
eBook edition: ISBN-13: 978-0-88050-437-9

Contents

Preface

W̶hen Osho spoke with his secretary about creating a book from selections of his talks titled, The Greatest Challenge: The Golden Future; *he gave detailed suggestions concerning subjects and issues he had spoken about that should be included. He specifically wanted the compilation to address the challenges of over-population and global warming, globalization and war, poverty and ecological devastation – challenges that we face today in an increasingly urgent way. This new edition expands on the material originally presented in that publication. Here is an excerpt from the original notes given by Osho:*

The future should not be just a hope and opportunity; those are just lousy words. The future should be absolutely ours – it should be a golden future. We have lived with the idea of a golden past – which was never golden! But we can create a future that is really golden.

Now is a great moment. We can manage to have one world. This crisis is a golden crisis, because people change only under conditions of such deep stress. As long as the situation is tolerable, people will tolerate it – but now we are at a point where the situation is not tolerable. There is no more time for commissions and their reports.

The problems are very simple. It is just that it has to be made clear to the whole humanity that these problems are your creation, and you are still creating them. A great awareness has to be spread: "These are the problems you are supporting. Withdraw your support."

And some practical steps should be taken … for example, if someone wants to be a world citizen, the United Nations should provide world citizen passports, not connected with any nation. Just small steps can have a large impact immediately, they will create an atmosphere. This crisis has been created by religions and nationalities, and it has come to the point where they cannot exist anymore.

If anything is to be done for the future, now is the time. Otherwise the greatest evolution of consciousness in the universe will disappear – and that is not only a loss to the earth, but to the whole of existence. In a million years we have been able to create some possibility of consciousness. But now we don't have time to wait for nature to go on developing in its slow way. It has eternity, but we don't have.

If we are going to solve the future and dissolve the problems, then we have to look for the roots in the past. It is our whole past, in all its dimensions, that has brought about this dangerous situation – and nobody talks about that, because no generation before this has ever bothered about the future. Man has always been living the way he wanted, and forced each new generation to live in the same way. This is no longer possible. We have to take a quantum leap – to teach the new generation not to live the same way we have lived. Only then can the future be shifted.

Introduction

This small book is unashamedly addressed to the intelligent people of this threatened planet. It is one man's vision for a viable humanity; it is one man's diagnoses of the psychological and social sicknesses that divide human beings, within and without, into warring factions. In this selection of texts from his talks, Osho outlines the changes he sees as critical if there is to be any future – and in particular, the golden future he knows is within our grasp.

The fact that the very survival of the planet is at stake is doubted by no one – yet, nothing changes. Every attempt to turn away from greed and exploitation, and build a sustainable future, is with met with resistance at every turn – and nothing changes. That we are sacrificing the very existence of the most beautiful flowering of this universe in childishly immature conflicts is widely understood – yet nothing changes. That action is needed now, is accepted by global experts everywhere – and nothing changes.

The clock keeps ticking, and the news keeps repeating itself, and even worsening… War, famine, AIDS … chemical weapons, holes in the ozone layer, nuclear weapons … global warming, overpopulation, loss of species… greed, violence, economic meltdown…

The tragic fact is that if the intelligent people of the earth don't stop this process, just who do they think will? The people in power, who currently benefit from today's insane world? The same tired politics, institutions, churches and "masters of the universe" who got us into this mess in the first place?

It is now or never. It is time for the intelligentsia everywhere to raise its voice against all these stupidities.

In this book, Osho offers a unique perspective on change – where it has to come from in order to be effective, why our efforts to bring about change have failed in the past, and what to expect by way of opposition from those whose interests are in maintaining the status quo. And he lays out a series of proposals for the practical steps we must take if we are to truly begin to heal the wounds of the planet, and build a new foundation for creating a paradise – right here, right now – on earth.

Many of his proposals are radical – these are radical times, and they call for radical solutions, It is not a question of whether you agree with Osho or not, it is a question of having the guts to ensure that at least his contribution is on the agenda. If the ideas are obviously wrong, then it will be easy to point out how and why, and we can all learn in the process. If the ideas are right, then we will need to find the courage to say so. Time is running out, and everything we love is at stake. Pretending you didn't hear a word is not an acceptable excuse.

This planet is the inheritance of every one of us. Either we all benefit or we all lose – it is one earth, and one humanity. It our search for survival we must leave no stone unturned. We must examine every option openly, honestly, without prejudice, without superstition, without bias – in fact, simply and scientifically.

Osho's vision is one set of options you will find nowhere else.

If it should turn out that we do lose this planet without having thoroughly investigated every avenue before us, Homo sapiens will have been the misnomer of the universe.

John Andrews
M.D., M.B., B.S.M.R.C

CHAPTER 1

From the Personal to the Political:
Changing Yourself, Changing the World

Everybody is born as one single individual, but by the time he is mature enough to participate in life he has become a crowd. But most people are not aware of it.

If you just sit silently and listen to your mind, you will find so many voices. You will be surprised, you can recognize those voices very well. Some voice is from your grandfather, some voice is from your grandmother, some voice is from your father, some voice is from your mother. Some voice is from the priest, from the teacher, from the neighbors, from your friends, from your enemies. All these voices are jumbled up in a crowd within you, and if you want to find your own voice it is almost impossible; the crowd is too thick.

In fact, you have forgotten your own voice long ago. You were never given freedom enough to voice your opinions. You were taught obedience, you were taught to say yes to everything your elders were saying to you. You were taught that you have to follow whatever your teachers or your priests are doing. Nobody ever told you to search for your own voice; nobody asked you, "Have you got any voice of your own or not?"

So your voice has remained very subdued and other voices are very loud, very commanding, because they were orders and you had followed them – in spite of yourself. You had no intention to follow, you could see that this is not right. But one has to be obedient to be respected, to be acceptable, to be loved.

Naturally only one voice is missing in you; only one person is missing in you, and that is you; otherwise there is a whole crowd. And that crowd is constantly driving you mad, because one voice says, "Do this," another voice says, "Never do that! Don't listen to that voice!" And you are torn apart.

This whole crowd has to be withdrawn. This whole crowd has to be told, "Now please leave me alone!" The people who have gone to the mountains or to secluded forests were really not going away from the society; they were trying to find a place where they could disperse their crowd inside. And those people who have made a place within you are obviously reluctant to leave.

But if you want to become an individual in your own right, if you want to get rid of this continuous conflict and this mess within you, then you have to say goodbye to them – even when they belong to your respected father, your mother, your grandfather. It does not matter to whom they belong. One thing is certain: they are not your voices. They are the voices of people who have lived in their time, and they had no idea what the future was going to be. They have loaded their children with their own experience; their experience is not going to match with the unknown future.

They think they are helping their children to be knowledgeable, to be wise, so their lives can be easier and more comfortable, but they are doing just the wrong thing. With all the good intentions in the world, they destroy the child's spontaneity, his own consciousness, his own ability to stand on his feet and to respond to the new future that their ancestors had no idea of.

Each child is going to face new storms, he is going to face new situations, and he needs a totally new consciousness to respond. Only then is his response is going to be fruitful; only then can he can have a victorious life, a life that is not just a long, drawn-out despair, but a dance from moment to moment, which goes on becoming more and more deep to the last breath. He enters into death dancing, and joyously.

Be silent, and find your own self.

Unless you find your own self, it is very difficult to disperse the crowd, because all those in the crowd are pretending, "I am your self." And you have no way to agree or disagree.

So don't create any fight with the crowd. Let them fight amongst themselves – they are quite efficient in fighting amongst themselves. You, meanwhile, try to find yourself. And once you know who you are, you can just order them to get out of the house – it is actually that simple! But first you have to find yourself.

Once *you* are there, the master is there. The owner of the house is there, and all these people, who have been pretending to be masters themselves, start dispersing. One who is himself, unburdened of the past, discontinuous with the past, original, strong as a lion and inno-cent as a child, can reach to the stars, or even beyond the stars; his future is golden.

Up to now people have always been talking about the golden past. We have to learn the language of the golden future.

There is no need for you to change the whole world; just change yourself and you have started changing the whole world, because you are part of the world. If even a single human being changes, that change will radiate to thousands and thousands of others. You will become a triggering point for a revolution which can give birth to a totally new kind of human being.

> *One part of me wants to sit relax, meditate, and focus*
> *on my own inner growth, but the other part has the drive*
> *to work, run around, organize, jump up and down, fight,*
> *talk to press and politicians, just shout from the rooftops.*
> *How can I resolve the contradiction between these two*
> *impulses?*

Man is both the inner and the outer, and it has been a fallacy, a very ancient fallacy, to condemn one in favor of the other.

In the East, people renounce the outer in favor of the inner. They escape from the world into the caves in the Himalayas so that they can devote their whole life and their whole time and their whole energy to the inner journey – but they don't understand the dialectics of life.

In the West, just the opposite has been done. They have renounced the inner so that they can put their whole energy into the outer world and the conquest of the outer world.

Both have been wrong, and both have been right.

Both have been wrong because both remained halves; one part grew bigger and bigger, and the other part remained stunted. You can see it.

In the East there is so much poverty, so much disease, so much sickness, so much death. Still, there is a certain contentment. With all this, there seems to be no revolutionary approach that "We should change the whole world. We cannot go on living in this poverty, and we have lived in this poverty for centuries, in slavery for centuries. And we have accepted everything – poverty, slavery, disease, death – without any resistance, because these are outer things. Our whole effort has been inner."

In the West they have destroyed poverty, they have destroyed much disease, they have made man's life longer. They have made man's body more beautiful, they have made man's existence more comfortable, but the man himself – for whom all these comforts, all these conquests of science and technology have been done – is missing. They have completely forgotten for whom it was done. The inside is hollow. Everything is there, all around, and in the middle there is a retarded consciousness, almost non-existential.

So both have succeeded in what they were doing, and both have failed – because they have chosen only half of man's life.

My attitude is that of accepting man in his totality, in his wholeness.

And it has to be understood that once you accept the totality of man, you have to understand the law of dialectics.

For example, the whole day you work hard in the fields, in the garden; you perspire. In the night you will have a beautiful sleep. Don't think that because the whole day you have been working so hard, how can you sleep in the night, because it is so against your whole day's work. It is not against it! The whole day's hard work has prepared you to relax; the night will be a deep relaxation.

Beggars sleep the best. Emperors cannot sleep because the emperor has forgotten the dialectics of life. You need two legs to walk, you need two hands, you need two hemispheres in your brain.

It has now become an accepted psychological truth that you can do hard mathematical work, because it is done by one part of the mind, and then you can do the same hard work on your musical instrument – and because it is done by another part of the mind, it is not continuous labor. In fact, when you are working hard on mathematics, the musical part of your mind is resting; and when you are working hard on the musical part, your mathematical mind is resting.

In the universities, in the colleges all over the world, we change the class period every forty minutes because it has been found that after each forty minutes, the part of the brain that you have been working with gets tired. Just change the subject, and that part goes into rest.

Sitting with me, fill your cup with as much juice as possible. Feel silence to its uttermost depth, so that you can shout from the housetops.

And there is no contradiction: your shouting from the housetops is simply part of a dialectical process. Your silence and your running around are just like two hands, your two legs, your day and night, your work and rest period. Don't divide them as antagonistic to each other; that's how the whole world has suffered.

The East has created great geniuses, but we are still living in the bullock cart age because our geniuses simply meditated. Their meditation never came into action. If they had meditated for a few hours and used their silence and peace and meditativeness for scientific research, India would have been the richest country in the world – outer and inner, both.

The same is true about the West: they created great geniuses, but they were all involved with things, objects. They forgot themselves completely. Once in a while a genius remembered, but it was too late. Albert Einstein, at the time of death, said his last words – and remember, the last words are the most important a person has ever spoken in his life, because they are a conclusion, the essential experience. His last words were, "If there is another life, I would like to be a plumber. I don't want to be a physicist. I want to be something very simple – a plumber."

A tired brain, a burned out brain…and what was his achievement? Hiroshima and Nagasaki. This man was capable of becoming a Gautam Buddha. If he had looked inwards, he had such an insight that perhaps he would have gone deeper than any Gautam Buddha, because he looked towards the stars and went further than any astronomer has ever done. It is the same power; it is only a question of direction.

But why get fixed? Why not keep yourself available to both dimensions? What is the need of getting fixed? "I can only see outwardly, I cannot see inwardly," or vice-versa. One should only learn how to see *deeply*, and then use that insight in both dimensions. Then he can give better science and better technology to the world and he can give better human beings, a better humanity, at the same time.

And remember, only in a better human being's hands is a better technology right; otherwise, it is dangerous.

The East is dying with poverty and the West is dying with power. They have created so much power that they can only kill. They don't know anything about life because they have never looked in. The East knows everything about life, but without food you cannot meditate. When you are hungry and you close your eyes, you can see only chapattis just floating all around!

It happened in the life of a poet, Heinrich Heine. He was lost in a jungle for three days, hungry, tired. Out of fear, he could not sleep; wild animals were staying in the tops of the trees in the night. And for three days continuously he did not come across a single human being to ask whether he was moving right or wrong, where he was going or if he was moving in a roundabout. Three days continuously...and then came the full moon night.

Hungry, tired, hanging onto a tree, he looked at the full moon. He was a great poet, and he was surprised, he could not believe it. He himself had written about the moon, he had read about the moon. So much is written about the moon – so much poetry, so much painting, so much art is around the moon. But Heinrich Heine had a revelation: before, he used to see his beloved's face in the moon; today he saw only a loaf of bread floating in the sky. He tried hard, but the beloved's face did not appear.

It is perfectly good to be dialectical. And always remember to try the opposites as complementaries. Use all the opposites as complementaries and your life will be fuller, your life will be whole.

To me, this is the only holy life: a whole life is the only holy life.

CHAPTER 2

In Search of Direction for Change:
To the Golden Past or a Golden Future?

The most important need of humanity today is to be made aware that its past has betrayed it. There is no point in continuing the past, it will be suicidal. A new humanity is absolutely and urgently needed.

The new humanity will not be a society in the old sense, where individuals are only parts of it. The new humanity will be a meeting of individuals, where individuals are the masters and society is to serve them. It will have many different aspects to it. It will not have so many religions, it will have only a religious consciousness. It will not have a despot God as a creator, because that implies the slavery of man. It will have godliness as a quality of ultimate achievement, a quality of enlightenment. God will be spread all over – in everything, in every being.

The individual, for the first time, will not be programmed; he will be helped to be himself. He will not be given any ideals, any discipline, any certain pattern. He will be given only a tremendous love for freedom, so that he can sacrifice everything, even his own life, but he cannot sacrifice freedom. The new individual will not be repressive; he will be natural, with no inhibitions, expressive of everything that he has. Just the way plants express themselves in different colors, in different fragrances, each individual will be doing the same.

The new individual will not have the false idea that all human beings are equal. They are not. They are unique, which is a far higher concept than equality. Although the new individuals will not be equal, they will have equal opportunity to develop their potential, whatever it is.

There will be no marriage; love will be the only law. Children will be part of the commune, and only the commune will decide who is capable of being a mother and who is capable of being a father. It cannot be at random and accidental. And it will be according to the needs of the earth.

The new humanity will have an ecology in which nature is not to be conquered, but lived and loved. We are part of it – how can we conquer it? It will not have any races, no distinctions between nations, between colors, castes. It will not have any nations, any states. It will have only a functional world government, and the world government will not be chosen by mediocre voters – because they necessarily chose people of their own category.

It will have a totally different pattern. Just as we don't allow anybody to vote before he is twenty-one years old – he has to be adult – in exactly the same way, unless everybody is well-educated and has at least a bachelor's degree, he will not be allowed to vote. And the people will vote, not for any party – because there will be no party at all, it will be a no-party system – people will vote directly for individuals.

An education minister, a foreign minister, an interior minister, a president – these people will stand on their individual merit. Just as no voter can have less than a bachelor's degree, nobody can stand for any post who does not have a doctorate in that particular subject. So all those who will be standing for the post will be experts on the same subject, and the choice will be by the educated, by the intelligent.

And the government will not be in the old sense a government. It won't have any power, it will be simply functional. It will be the servant of the society in the real sense, not only in words.

Life has so many dimensions, and politics has dominated them all. Looking at a newspaper, somebody on some other planet could not conceive what kind of people live on the earth – only politicians? murderers?

suicides? rapists? criminals?...because your newspapers are full of these people, and on top of everything is the politician.

Every creative dimension of life will be brought out into the light, and the ugly aspects don't need to be advertised. If somebody has murdered, it should be brought to light – not to say that he was a criminal, but to show how the very psychology of the man, the upbringing of the man went wrong, and why he had to commit murder. In his place, with the same background, anybody would have done the same. So you are not condemning the person, you are condemning the training, the background, the upbringing; this is absolutely scientific.

Why does a man become a rapist? – because his background was creating the energy to be a rapist. He was trying to be a Baptist, but he ended up being a rapist! So the negative part should be brought out, but the individual should never be condemned because no action is equal to the whole individual. The action is a small part of his whole life.

The newspapers should be full of creativity, positivity. Ninety percent of a newspaper should give coverage to musicians, poets, sculptors, dancers, actors, philosophers and only ten percent should be given to the politicians and negative elements. The negative elements should be analyzed, so the individual is not condemned. And the politicians should only be given space as information, not more than that. If they are doing something good it should be said, if they are doing something not good it should be said – but they should not be dominating our whole life.

The new humanity will have to change the whole structure of its education. It will not be ambitious, it will not create a desperate desire in everybody to become somebody powerful. On the contrary, it will create creators. It will create people who know how to rejoice. Its basic function should be to teach people the art of living, loving, laughing, the capacity to sing, dance, paint.

There will be people who have to be trained for technology, science, but even those who are being trained for technology and science or medicine should not be kept completely unconscious of the beautiful side of life. They should not become robots – because what you do, you become. If you are continuously researching objects, soon you forget that you are a subject; you become an object, too.

And each individual who enters a school, college, or university should have sessions in which he can be encouraged to meditate – so meditation comes from within him, it is not imposed from the outside. It is not required to meditate, the desire to meditate is coming from the inside. Things like meditation cannot be forced; then there is resentment. But meditation can help man drop all kinds of resentment, all kinds of jealousies, hatred, competition. It can clean man's inner shrine so completely that everybody grows up and does not only grow old.

A new man is an absolute necessity. The old is dead or is dying, it cannot survive long. And if we cannot produce a new human being, then humanity will disappear from the earth.

> *To me the future appears bleak whichever way one looks at it – either poverty and starvation, or Westernization through capitalism – for is it not necessary for people to become materially rich before they become interested in the inner search? But the burden of the Western capitalism already lies heavy on the world: the atomic bomb; violence through frustration; the mechanical nature of most people's lives,; the destruction of the forests and the pollution of the air and sea so that it is uncertain whether the environment can maintain its delicate balance. How can the planet possibly survive all this?*

The future appears bleak, yes…but it has always appeared so. This is not anything new. You can go as far back as possible in human history, to the very first moment of human beginnings when Adam and Eve were expelled from the garden of Eden, and you will find the future has always looked bleak. Just think of Adam and Eve being thrown out of the God's garden and the doors being slammed behind them. How was the future? It must have appeared very bleak. All that they had known was being taken away. Their security, their safety, their world, everything was being taken away. What future hope was there? Only darkness, death. It must have been frightening.

And this is not just a parable: each time a child is born the future looks bleak, because again the garden, the womb – the safe, secure environment of the womb – is taken away from the child, and the helpless child is expelled. How do you think the child feels? Psychoanalysts say that the greatest trauma is the birth trauma, and the person suffers from it his whole life. The word "trauma" comes from a root which means "wound". The birth trauma is the greatest wound; it is very rare to find a person whose birth trauma is healed. It heals only when a person becomes enlightened, because when a person becomes enlightened he is again in the eternal womb of God; otherwise the wound goes on and on hurting.

Your whole life you try to hide that wound, but by hiding it, it cannot disappear. Each child being born, coming out of the birth canal, must be feeling the future is bleak. And each age has felt it, because the future is unknown – that's why it looks bleak.

This is not something new that modern man is feeling; it is as ancient as man. You can go to the ancient-most records and it is always said in every ancient scripture, "The future is bleak." And the corollary to it is that the past was golden. "The future is bleak." The past was good, *satyug*, the Age of Truth; the future, *kalyug*, was the Age of Death and Darkness.

This attitude is somewhere deep in everybody's mind; it has nothing to do with time and the realities surrounding you. And you have to drop this pessimistic attitude.

It all depends on your approach.

For example, in the past we could have continued to have wars between the big powers in the world because our wars were so inefficient, there was no danger. That's why, down the ages, in three thousand years we have fought five thousand wars. There was no problem; it was just a game. And the male egoistic mind has enjoyed it very much, it has needed it very much. These types of wars would have continued if there was no atom bomb. Its very existence means that now, if you decide for war, it will be universal suicide. Who is ready to take that risk? Nobody can win and everybody will die. If nobody can be the winner; then what is the point of the game? War is significant if somebody can win and somebody is defeated. It becomes absurd if nobody can win and both are destroyed. Because of the existence of the atom bomb the big powers in the world are prevented from going to war with each other. It is ridiculous now to go to war. If all parties are going to be destroyed, then what is the point? The atom bomb has made war pointless. When I think about the atom bomb I see great hope. I am not a pessimist at all. I believe things are going to be better every day, better and better. You will be surprised, but this is so simple if you understand.

It is because of the atom bomb that war has become total. Before the bomb it was a partial thing – a few people will die – but now the whole earth will die. We have so many bombs ready that we can kill each person a thousand times, we can destroy a thousand earths like this. This earth is small now in the face of our destructive powers; compared to our destructive powers this earth is nothing. Now who is going to take this risk, and for what? You will not be there to gloat over your victory – nobody will be there.

The Third World War is not going to happen. And it will not be because of Buddha and Christ and their teachings of non-violence and love, no! It will be because of the atom bomb – because death is absolute now, the suicide will be complete. Not only will man be destroyed, but birds, animals, trees, all life will be destroyed on earth.

This is the only possibility of dropping war forever. We have become too efficient in killing; now killing can be allowed no more. Think this way and you will be surprised – then the future is no longer bleak.

Yes, you can become frustrated and you can become violent because all that you have hoped for has failed – you have succeeded and nothing has succeeded, so great frustration arises in you. You can become murderous, you can become suicidal. But the other possibility is also there: You can start thinking in a totally new way. You can start thinking that success cannot be found in the outer world, that success has to be about something inner, that you have been rushing in a wrong direction. Your direction was wrong; that's why you have failed.

Because of frustration, people become more and more interested in meditation, prayer, contemplation. My own observation is a person becomes a meditator only when there are only two possibilities: suicide or transformation. When in the outside world there seems to be only suicide and nothing else, then one turns in. Only at that point, at that peak of frustration, does one turn in. The turning in cannot happen in a lukewarm person; it happens only when things are really hot and there is no way outside anymore, all ways have been proved false. When you have been frustrated totally by the outside world and all exterior journeys, when all extroversion seems meaningless, only then does the desire, the longing for an inner pilgrimage open up.

It has always been so. It is only at the extremes, when life faces a crisis, that transformations happen. Water evaporates at a hundred degrees; that much heat is needed. When there is that much heat of frustration a few people will become violent, a few people will become murderous, a few people will become suicidal, but the major part of humanity will start turning in.

And it is not that industrialization and the growth of technology has made man mechanical, has made man a machine. Man has always been a machine. Industrialization has only revealed the truth, and it is a great revelation. Man has always lived in slavery, but the slavery was not so apparent, was not so penetrating; there was always an illusion of freedom.

The mechanization of all that you are surrounded with has made you aware that you are also nothing but a machine. You have always been that! Buddhas have always been telling you that you exist unconsciously, that you exist like a robot, that you are not yet a human being, but your illusions persisted. The modern world has taken the last illusion from you, it has revealed the truth to you: that you are nothing but a machine – efficient, inefficient, but a machine.

It had to be so, because only when you live with machines can you become aware of your machine-like existence. You had always lived with trees and animals and people in the past, and it had always given you the false idea that there was freedom.

Freedom exists only when you are utterly conscious. Only a buddha is free. Freedom is in buddhahood; nobody else is free, nobody else can be free. But people can believe they are free, and it is a very consoling illusion. The modern world has taken your illusion away from you; and it is good because now a great desire to be free will arise, a great longing to attain to something beyond the machine.

For example, the computer has proved that howsoever efficient you are in your mind it is not the mind that makes really human, because that work can be done better by a computer. The people who used to do beautiful mathematics will be offended because the computer can do it in a far better way. And the work of the computer is such, they say that if a problem will take seventy years for a great mathematician to solve, working day in, day out, the computer can solve it within a second.

Now, what is the lesson to be learned? That the brain is nothing but a bio-computer. Without the computer it would never have been revealed to you that your brain is a computer. With the computer, now, the people who think they are great intellectuals, mathematicians, scientists, specialists, are all reduced to machines. It was not possible two thousand years before: there was no way to know that the mind functions as a machine, that the mind is nothing but a machine.

There is just one thing the computer cannot do. It can be logical but it cannot be loving; it can be rational, but it cannot be meditative.

A computer cannot meditate, a computer cannot love – and that is the hope, and that is where man can still go beyond machines. You can love. Your love will be the decisive factor in the coming days, not logic. The computer is perfectly logical, more logical than any Aristotle. Not mathematics – the computer is more mathematical than any Albert Einstein.

The computer is going to solve all those types of problems. The computer will solve every problem that scientists used to take years to solve. It can solve them within seconds. Sooner or later science will go into the hands of computers and the scientist will be needed only to operate the computer, that's all. The computer can do so many things far more quickly, far more efficiently, with less and less possibility of making any errors.

This is something tremendously significant. It can make you very frightened, it can give you the idea that there is nothing left, that man is just a machine... but it can also fill you with great hope because now the computer has revealed that the head is not man's true reality.

Now we have to search for the heart, because the computer has no heart. Only by searching for our heart, only by allowing our heart to dance and sing and love, will we be able to retain the glory and dignity of being human; otherwise it is gone.

The future looks bleak to you because you only see the darker side of the phenomenon. You are not aware of its lighter side. I see the dawn coming very close. Yes, the night is very dark – but the future is not bleak, not at all.

In fact, for the first time in human history millions of people will be able to become buddhas. It was very rare to become a buddha in the past because it was very rare to become aware of the mechanicalness of man. It needed great intelligence to be aware that man is a machine. But now it will not need any intelligence at all; it will be so obvious.

And you say, "…the destruction of the forests and the pollution of the air and sea so that it is uncertain whether the environment can maintain its delicate balance. How can the world possibly survive all this?" That is one of the most beautiful things about science and technology: it creates problems just to solve them. And the problem can only be solved when it has been created; then it becomes a challenge. Now the greatest challenge before technology is how to maintain the balance of nature, how to maintain ecological harmony. That challenge was never there before, it is a new problem.

For the first time science is facing a new problem. We have lived on this earth for millions of years. Slowly, slowly we had been growing more and more expert technologically, but we had not yet been able to destroy the natural balance; we were as yet a very small force on the earth. Now for the first time our energy is bigger, far bigger, than the earth's energy to keep its balance. This is a great phenomenon. Man has become so powerful that he can destroy the natural balance. But he will not destroy it, because to destroy the natural balance means he will be destroyed himself.

He will find new ways – and new ways are being found. The way to regain the delicate balance of nature is not by renouncing technology. It is not by becoming hippies, it is not by becoming Gandhians, no, not at all. The way to regain the balance of nature is through superior technology, higher technology, more technology. If technology can destroy the balance, why can't technology regain it? Anything that can be destroyed can be created.

And now it is almost feasible to float cities in the sky, in the air, in big, enormous balloons! There is no need for everybody to live on the earth. And it will be really beautiful – floating cities in the air, and the green earth below you, huge forests again as the earth used to be before we started cutting all the forests. The earth can become the same again. You can come back to the earth for holidays.

It is possible now to float cities in the ocean, and that will be beautiful. It is possible now to make underground cities so the earth, its greenery, its beauty, is not destroyed. You can live in air-conditioned cities underneath the earth. You can come once in a while for your Sunday prayer to the earth, and go back. It is possible for man now to be transported to another planet. The moon may become our next colony, the moon may become our habitation.

The way is not by regressing; it is not possible to regress. Now man cannot live without electricity and man cannot live without all the comforts that technology has made available. And there is no need either – it would become so poor a world. You don't know how people lived in the past, always starving, always ill. You have forgotten. In the past, if twenty children were born only two would survive. Life was very ugly.

And without machines there was slavery. It is only because of machines that slavery has disappeared from the earth. If more machines come, then more of this slavery will disappear. Horses become free again if more cars are there; oxen become free again if more machines are there to do their work; animals can become free again.

Freedom was not possible without machines. If you drop machines, people will again become slaves. There will be those who will start dominating and forcing. You see the pyramids? They look so beautiful, but each pyramid was made in such a way that millions of people died in making it. That was the only way to build those big structures. All the beautiful palaces of the world, and the forts… So much violence happened, only in that way could they be made. The Great Wall of China – millions of people died in making it. They were forced, generations of people were forced to just make this China Wall. Now people go and see it, and they have completely forgotten that it represents such an ugly chapter of history.

For the first time electricity and technology have taken on the work; man need not do it. Technology can free man absolutely from work and the earth can be playful for the first time. Luxury is possible for the first time. There is no need to go back.

That's why I am against the Gandhian approach towards life, utterly against. If Gandhi is followed, then the world will again become ugly, poor, dirty, ill. The way is ahead: one has to go to superior technology that can restore the balance. The earth can really become paradise.

I am all for science. My vision is not against science; my vision absorbs science in itself. I believe in a scientific world. And through science a great religion, a greater religion than ever, is going to happen to man, because when man can be really free to be playful and there is no need to work, tremendous creativity will be released. People will paint, and people will play music, and people will dance, and people will write poems, and people will meditate. Their whole energy will be free to soar high.

Only a small part of humanity has been creative, because all the other people have been forced to do futile things that can be done by machines more easily and without any trouble to anybody. Millions of people are simply laboring their whole lives. Their whole lives consist only of perspiration, there is no inspiration. This is ugly, this should not be.

And this is possible only for the first time.

Just think…the whole of humanity freed from the imprisonment of labor; then the energy will start moving in new directions. People will become adventurers, explorers, scientists, musicians, poets, painters, dancers, meditators. They will have to because the energy will need some expression. Millions of people can bloom like buddhas.

I am tremendously hopeful about the future.

You say, "To me the future appears bleak whichever way one looks at it." It is not bleak. It can be bleak if stupidity wins over intelligence. If the old, rotten mind wins over intelligence – then it is bleak. If Gandhi wins, then it is bleak. If stupid politicians and dictators win, then it is bleak. But if I am heard and understood it is not bleak.

You say, "…either poverty and starvation, or Westernization through capitalism." I am all for Westernization and I am all for capitalism too, because capitalism is the only natural system. Communism is a violent, enforced, artificial system. Capitalism is a natural growth; nobody has forced it on anybody, it has come on its own. It is part of human evolution. Capitalism is not like communism, with a few people trying to enforce a particular system on others. Capitalism has grown out of freedom. Capitalism is a natural phenomenon, and it fits perfectly well with human potentials. I am all in favor of Adam Smith and all against Karl Marx.

Capitalism means laissez-faire. People should be free to do their own thing; no government should interfere with people's freedom. The government that governs the least is the best. That's what capitalism is. The interference of the state, the nationalization of industries, are all inhuman. Communism can exist only in a climate of dictatorship. Communism cannot be democratic, socialism can never be democratic. No socialist can have the democratic mind, because socialism or communism means to impose a particular system on people. How can you be democratic? It has to be forcibly imposed; the whole country has to be turned into a concentration camp.

Capitalism needs no enforcement from above, it is a democratic way of life. And capitalism is also psychologically truer, because no two persons are psychologically equal. The whole idea of equality is false, inhuman, untrue, unscientific. No two human beings are equal; people are unequal. In every possible way they are unequal. Their talents, their intelligence, their bodies, their health, their age, their beauty, their qualities – everything is different No two individuals are alike or equal.

And it is good! The variety makes life rich; the variety gives people individuality, uniqueness.

Capitalism means freedom, it represents freedom. I am not against equal opportunities for all – please, don't misunderstand me. Equal opportunities should be available to everybody. But for what? – equal opportunities to grow to your unequal potentials, equal opportunities to be different, to be dissimilar, equal opportunities to be whatsoever you want to be.

Communism destroys human freedom in the name of equality. And the equality can never be managed, there is no possible way. Even in Soviet Russia there was no equality; only the classes changed their labels. First there used to be the proletarians and the bourgeoisie; then there were the rulers and the ruled, and the distinctions were far greater than ever. The whole country fell into a kind of dull state.

Communism makes people drab and dull, placid, because nobody feels the freedom to be himself, so joy disappears from life. Nobody feels any enthusiasm to work for others. That is unnatural, inhuman. How can you feel enthusiasm if you are working for the inhuman state, the machinery called the state? When you work for your children, your wife, there is enthusiasm. If you are working for your wife and you would like her to have a beautiful house, a small cottage in the hills, you have great enthusiasm. You would like your children to be healthy; you have great enthusiasm. Who cares for the state? For what? The state is an abstraction; nobody can love the state. Communism, in the beautiful name of equality, destroys the most valuable thing – freedom. Freedom is the ultimate value. There is nothing higher than freedom, because it is through freedom that everything else becomes possible.

I am all for capitalism. Capitalism functions in a totally different way. It helps you to express, to manifest, to flower in your totality.

And I am not saying that there are not wrong things in capitalism. They are there – but capitalism is not responsible for them. Human ignorance is responsible for them, human unconsciousness is responsible for them. Capitalism has many errors in it; it is not the perfect system. It is the most perfect in available systems, but it is not the perfect system, because man is not perfect. It simply reflects man, with all its illusions, with all human errors, with all human stupidities…but it reflects perfectly well.

Communism is an effort to live by bread alone. Bread is needed, but it is needed only so that you can can sing a song, so that you can fall in love, so that you can paint. Bread is needed, but only as a means. Communism has turned the means into the end.

I am in favor of the world being Westernized because Westernization means nothing but modernization. Forget the word "West". Westernization means modernization: more technology, more science, and higher technology so that we can save this earth and its delicate ecological balance. The world to be modernized, and then the future is not bleak.

But the greatest problem is that the old mind is against modernization. The old traditions are great blocks. The conditioning of the old, traditional mind is such that people are committing suicide. They think that they have great culture and great values and great ideas...and it is all rotten! And because of that rotten past, they cannot understand the modern explosion of great knowledge that can transform this earth into a real paradise.

These old patterns have to be destroyed.

People ask me, particularly Indians, "What are you doing to help India to get out of its poverty?" That's actually what I am doing, because to me it is not only a question of going and distributing clothes to poor people; that is not going to help. It is not a question of distributing anything, it is not a question of charity; it is a question of changing their mind and their structure of thinking. But then the problem arises: they will be the most antagonistic to me. This is how life is paradoxical. What I am saying can change the fate of the East, it can transform its whole ugliness into beauty, but the Eastern people will be the most against me because whatsoever I will say will go against their conditioning, their ideas – settled ideas, of centuries. That's why you don't see many Indians here.

The Western mind immediately feels a deep attunement with me. It is because I am always in favor of the modern, of the new. The Western mind can understand me immediately, it feels a great affinity, but the Eastern mind simply feels agitated. The moment the Eastern mind hears what I am saying he becomes annoyed, antagonistic; he starts defending himself.

He has become too attached to his mind, and his mind is the cause of all his problems. He wants to change those problems, but he clings to the mind. And that is not possible. First the mind has to be changed; only then will those problems disappear.

For example, the whole East suffers from repressed sexuality, great repression, but again and again they go on insisting that they have great ideas of celibacy, great ideas of character, morality. And those are the ideas which are making them repressed. Those are the ideas that are keeping them unflowing, because once your sexuality is repressed, your creativity is repressed, because sex energy is your creative energy. It is nature's way of helping you becoming creative. Sex is creativity. The man who has repressed his sex will not be able to create anything; he will be stuck.

Now what to do? If you tell them to become a little more loving, a little more sensuous, a little more sensate, they immediately are against you; they say, "Then why has Buddha said this, and Mahavira has said that? You are teaching materialism! "

I am simply teaching you totality. And let me say it to you, that Buddha's approach is not total, it is partial. But I can understand him, because if you are against me, now, twenty-five centuries after Buddha, if Buddha had said these things that I am saying to you, how much would you have been against him? I can understand why he never told you about the total growth of human beings, why he had to remain partial. Even that was too much for the Indian people, and Buddhism was thrown out of the country even that was too much. If he had talked the way I am talking, you would have immediately killed him. It was not possible; the climate was not ready for him to talk to you in total terms.

I am taking the risk of talking to you in total terms – and creating unnecessary troubles for myself! I can also go on teaching the old, stupid kind of spirituality, and India will be very proud of me and they will worship me. But I am not interested in being worshiped, and I am not interested in India being proud of me. My whole interest is how to change the country's rotten mind, how to give it a new vision.

And don't be worried that if more technology and industry is brought to the world, then the ecology will be destroyed. Don't be worried. Technology itself can find ways to overcome all those things. Technology is the only potential means in the hands of man to trans-form the outer world. The outer world can be transformed totally. We can bring it to an even better ecological balance than nature itself, because nature's ways are very primitive and rudimentary. And what is man really? – nature's highest growth. If man cannot bring a better balance, then who is going to bring it? Man is nature's highest peak; it is through man that nature can resettle its own problems.

I don't think that the future is bleak. The future is very hopeful, very bright. It has never been so before, because for the first time man is coming closer and closer to a point where he can be freed from all work. Man for the first time can live in luxury, and to live in luxury is to be ready to move inwards, because then there is no hindrance on the outside. Then you can simply move inwards, you will have to move inwards: the outer journey is finished. All that can be attained in the outside world has been attained…now a new adventure.

What happened to Buddha can happen to the whole of humanity in the future. He lived in luxury – he was the son of a king – and because of that luxurious living he became aware. Because there was no problem on the outside, he could relapse into himself, he could find ways and means to enter inwards. He became interested in knowing "Who am I?" What happened to Buddha can happen to the whole of humanity if the whole of humanity becomes rich, outwardly rich. To be outwardly rich is the beginning of inward richness.

And I teach an approach to religion that implies science in it, and I teach a religiousness that is sensate, sensuous. I teach a religiousness that accepts the body, loves the body, respects the body. I teach a religiousness that is earthly, earthy, which loves this beautiful earth, which is not against the earth. The earth has to be the base of your heavenly flight.

CHAPTER 3

Three Approaches to Change: Reform, Revolution, or Rebellion

Man's evolution passes through three stages: the reform, the revolution and the rebellion. The reform is the most superficial: it only touches the surface, it never goes more than skin-deep. It changes nothing but the window dressing of man; it changes the formalities. It gives man etiquette, manners – a kind of civilization – without changing anything essential in his being. It paints people, it polishes them, and yet deep down they remain the same. It is an illusion, it is fiction. It gives respectability, and makes everybody a hypocrite. It gives good manners, but they are against the inner core. The inner core has not even been understood. But for the society, reform creates smoothness.

Reform functions like a lubricant. It keeps the status quo going, it helps things remain the same – which will look paradoxical, because the reformist claims that he is changing society, but in fact all that he does is paint the old society in new colors. And the old society can exist more easily in new colors than it could have ever done with the old ones. The old were getting rotten; reform is a kind of renovation. The house is falling; the supports are falling, the foundations are shaking, and you go on giving new props to it, and in this way you can keep the house from falling a little longer. Reform is in the service of the status quo: it serves the past not the future.

The second approach is revolution; it goes a little deeper. Reform only changes ideas, it does not even change policies. Revolution goes deeper and touches the structure – but only the outer not the inner.

Man lives on two planes: one is the physical, the other is the spiritual. The revolution only goes to the physical structure – the economic, the political, they belong to the physical plane. It goes deeper than reform, it destroys many old things and creates many new things; but the being, the innermost being of man still remains unchanged. Revolution deals with morality, it deals with character. Reform deals with manners, etiquette, civilization, with changing the formal behavior of the person. Revolution changes the outer structures, and really changes them. It brings a new structure, but the inner blueprint remains the same; the inner consciousness is not touched. Revolution creates a split.

The first approach, the reform, creates hypocrisy. The second approach, the revolution, creates schizophrenia, it creates unbridgeable divisions. Man starts falling into two beings, and the bridge is broken. That's why revolutionaries go on denying the soul – Marx and Engels, Lenin and Stalin and Mao, all go on denying the soul. They have to deny it, they can't accept it because if they accept it then their whole revolution seems to be superficial, then it becomes apparent that their revolution is not total.

The reformist does not deny the soul, remember. He accepts it because it creates no problem for him – he never goes deeply enough to get to that point. Gandhi accepts the soul – he is a reformist. Reformists never say no to anything, they are people who go on saying yes; they are polite people. Unless it becomes absolutely necessary they will not reject anything, they will accept all. But revolutionaries deny the soul. They have to deny it, otherwise their revolution looks partial.

The third approach is rebellion. Rebellion is from the very essential core: it changes consciousness, it is radical; it transmutes, it is alchemical. It gives you a new being, not only a new body, not only new clothes, but a new being. A new man is born.

In the history of consciousness there have been three types of thinkers: the reformer, the revolutionary and the rebel. Manu, Moses, Gandhi – these are reformers, the most superficial. John the Baptist, Marx, Freud – these are the revolutionaries. And Jesus, Buddha, Krishnamurti – these are the rebels.

To understand rebellion is to understand the heart of religiousness. Religiousness is rebellion, it is utter change. Religiousness is a discontinuity with the past, the beginning of the new, the dropping of the old in its totality. Nothing has to be continued, because if something continues it will keep the old alive.

Reform paints the surface. Revolution destroys the old outer structure but the inner structure remains the same. In post-revolutionary communist societies the inner man has remained the same, there has been no difference, not a bit. They have had the same mind – the same greedy, ambitious, egoistic mind; the same mind that is found in America or in capitalist countries. But the outer structure of the society has been changed. The outer structure of laws, state, economics, politics – that has been changed. And once the police force, the governmental power is taken away, people will fall back to their old patterns again. The centralized, post-revolutionary society can be managed only by force, it cannot become democratic, because to allow people to be independent will be allowing them to bring their inner being again into their lives. And the inner being is still there – but they have been prevented, they have been obstructed; they cannot live it. They have to live by what the government says, they cannot live according to their being.

So communist societies have been basically dictatorial. And they will remain dictatorial, because the fear is that if man is given freedom, then because his consciousness is there – the greed is there, the ambition is there, and all that has always been is there – it will start working again. People will become rich and poor, powerful and powerless. People will start exploiting each other, people will start fighting for their ambitions. Of course, those who are powerful in those societies are still doing the same. Khrushchev used to brag about his cars, because he had so many. Nobody else could have them in Russia, but everybody wanted to have a car. It was just an enforcement, not real revolution.

Real revolution is spontaneous. That revolution is called rebellion.

A few more distinctions between these three words, then you will be able to understand my approach.

Reform does not require much from you. It says, "Just make your front door beautiful." You can let the whole house be dirty. You live in dirt, just don't allow your neighbors to see the dirt. But the front porch should be beautiful, because your neighbors are not interested in your inner being, in your inner house. They pass by the outside and they see only the front door. Do whatever you want, but do it at the back door. So the front door becomes a facade, a window, a showcase for the neighbors to see. You live at the back door really, you don't live at the front door. The front door is just there, artificial; you never enter through it, you never go out through it – it is there just to be seen by others.

Look at your front doors – everybody has them. They are called faces, masks, personalities because they are persona: lipstick and powder and cosmetics, they give you a persona. You are not that, it is just make-up.

Revolution goes a little deeper, but only a little deeper. It changes your drawing room so you can invite people in to sit there. In India it happens very often. In India the drawing room is beautiful, but don't go beyond that! People's kitchens are so dirty and ugly, their bathrooms are almost impossible. But nobody takes care of the bathroom or the kitchen; the only care that is taken is of the drawing room. It is there where you meet your guests.

This is false; it does not touch your real being, but it maintains your prestige. That's what morality is; it is a beautiful drawing-room. And if you can afford it, you can even have a Picasso painting in your drawing-room. It depends on how much you can afford.

Just the other day I was reading a small story:

Charlie was taking his out-of-town pal, George, for a stroll through the city. They were admiring the scenery when George observed, "Say, will you look at that good-looking girl over there? She's smiling at us. Do you know her?'

"Yes, that's Betty – twenty dollars."

"And who is that brunette with her? Man, she's really stacked!"

"Dolores – forty dollars."

"Ah, but look what's coming! That's what I call really first-class."

"Gloria – eighty dollars."

"My God!" cried George. "Aren't there any nice, respectable girls in this town?"

"Of course," Charlie answered. "But you couldn't afford their rates."

Morality goes only so far, beyond that it stumbles and disappears. Everybody has his price. The moral man has a price. Watch yourself – if you are walking on the street and you find a thousand dollars, maybe you will try to find the owner. But if you find ten thousand, then you hesitate…to try and find the person or not? If you find one hundred thousand dollars, then there is no question, you take them for yourself. That shows how deep your morality is – one thousand, ten thousand, one hundred thousand, everybody has a price. One can only afford that much, beyond that it is too much to sacrifice. The morality is not worth it! Then you would like to be immoral.

The moral person is not totally moral; only a few layers are moral, beyond that the immorality is waiting. So you can drive any moral person into immorality very easily. The only question is that you have to find out the price.

I have heard that Mulla Nasruddin was traveling with a woman in a first-class compartment. They were alone. He introduced himself, and then he said, "Would you like to sleep with me tonight?'

The woman became really angry, and said, "What do you think? Are you mad? What do you think of me? I am not a prostitute!"

Mulla said, "I could give you ten thousand dollars."

The woman started smiling, she came close, she was holding Mulla's hand.

And then Mulla said, "What about ten dollars?"

And the woman again said, "What do you think of me!"

Mulla said, "I know what you are. Now we are haggling over the price."

It is always a question of the price. Ten dollars and the woman is angry. Ten thousand dollars and the woman is willing. And don't laugh at her, this is the situation of everybody. Morality does not transform you. It goes deeper than reform, it has a bigger price, but still, at the very core of your being you remain the same.

Reform is partial revolution. Revolution is outer revolution. Rebellion is inner revolution. And only when the inner has happened, is it dependable; otherwise it is not dependable. Reform will make you a hypocrite, revolution will make you a schizophrenic. Only rebellion can give you your fullness of being, spontaneity, health, wholeness.

Reform will make you respectable. If you are after respect, then reform is enough. It will give you a plastic personality. From the outside you will start looking beautiful. From the inside you will be rotten and stinking, but nobody will be able to smell your stinking being; the plastic will protect you. Inside you will go on getting dirtier and dirtier, but on the outside you will keep a good face.

Revolution will create a split in you. It will make you a saint, but the sinner will be repressed. The sinner has not been absorbed into the saint, the sinner has been cut off. Revolution will make you two persons: it will create two worlds in you. The natural will be repressed and the moral will be on top of it. The top dog, the moral person, will try to control the underdog, the natural person. And of course, the natural is very powerful because it is natural! So it will take revenge; it will go on sneaking into your life through any weak points it can find. It will disrupt your morality, it will create guilt, and you will be in constant conflict because nobody can be victorious over the natural.

Your support, your intellectual support, is for the moral – but your whole being's support is for the natural. The moral is in the conscious, and the natural is in the unconscious. The conscious is very small, and the unconscious is nine times stronger, nine times bigger than the conscious. But you only know the conscious, so in the conscious mind the morality will go on singing its song, and in the unconscious, which is nine times more powerful, all kinds of immoralities will go on growing deeper roots in you. It will make you a saint *and* a sinner – the sinner will be repressed, and the sinner will wait for the right time to erupt, for the right time to take revenge.

That's why people look so sad, people look so dissipated because their whole energy is going down the drain in this conflict. Continuous tension is there. The saint is very tense, he is always in anguish and always afraid – afraid of his own being that he has denied. And the denied is still there! Sooner or later it will throw off the moralist, the egoist, the conscious pretender. It will overthrow the pretender.

The saint is always on the verge of a kind of insanity. And you know it…whenever you try to be a saint, you know that you are always on the verge. A small thing can change your whole balance, you can lose all your sanity. Neurosis breeds in you, grows, if you are split.

Rebellion is inner revolution. Rebellion starts from the "in," reform starts from the "out." Never start from the outside. Start from the innermost core. Start from your very being.

Reform will tell you what to do. Revolution will tell you how to be more saintly, of a better character, how to have good qualities. Revolution will make a hard crust around you, an armor that protects you from the outside and from the inside too. A hard, steel armor – that is what is called "character."

A real human being has no character. Jesus had no character, that was the problem, otherwise the Jews would not have been so much against him . He was liquid; he had no character, he had no armor. He was open, vulnerable, defenseless, because he was not a moralist. He was not a saint, he was a sage.

Reform makes you a gentleman. Revolution makes you a saint. Rebellion makes you a sage. Jesus was a sage, Buddha was a sage. Whatsoever they did was not done because of a certain morality, but because of a certain understanding; not because of rules given from the past, but because of a spontaneous awareness.

Rebellion depends on awareness, revolution on character, reform on formalities.

Start by being more aware, then you start from the innermost. Let the light spread from there, so your whole being can be full of light. There is no way to go from the outside. The only way is to come from the inside – just like a seed grows from the inside, sprouts from the inside and becomes a big tree. Let that be your inner work too – like a seed, grow.

Reform is patchwork, a kind of whitewash – a little bit here, a little bit there, but the basic structure is not even touched. Reform can be for revolution or can be against revolution; it depends on you. There are two types of reformists: those who are preparing the ground for revolution or those who are trying to prevent the revolution. Reform gives the feeling that things are getting better, so what is the need of creating a revolution? Why go to that much trouble? Reform gives hope, and people stop trying to rebel. So it depends on you.

A person of right understanding can use reform also, but one who is not conscious will not be able to use reform as a means for revolution – on the contrary, reform will become a hindrance for revolution. And so is the case with revolution. Revolution can be a door to rebellion, but only with awareness; otherwise it becomes a hindrance. One thinks, "Now the revolution has happened, what is the need to go any deeper? It is already too much."

So reform can either be a hindrance or a help. The same is the case with revolution. All depends on your awareness, all depends on your understanding – how much you understand life.

So let this become one of the most fundamental rules of life and work: that everything ultimately depends on understanding, on how deeply you understand. Even something that was going to become a great help can become a hindrance if understanding is missing. And even sometimes that which was going to be poisonous, with understanding can be changed into something medicinal. All medicines are made of poisons: they don't kill, they help people to remain healthy. In the right hands even poison becomes medicine; and in the wrong hands, even medicine may prove to be a poison.

Is renouncing the world and society part of a rebellious spirit?

The whole past is full of people who have renounced the world and society. Renunciation has become part of almost all religions, a foundational principle. But the rebel is renouncing the past. He is not going to repeat the past; he is bringing something new into the world.

Those who have renounced the world and society are escapists. They have really renounced their responsibilities, without understanding that the moment you renounce responsibilities you also renounce freedom. These are the complexities of life: freedom and responsibilities go away together or remain together.

The more you are a lover of freedom, the more you will be ready to accept responsibilities. But outside the world, outside the society, there is no possibility of any responsibility. And it has to be remembered that all that we learn, we learn through being responsible.

The past has destroyed the beauty of the word "responsibility." They have made it almost equivalent to duty; it is not really so. A duty is something done reluctantly, as part of your spiritual slavery. Duty to your elders, duty to your husband, duty to your children – they are not responsibilities. To understand the word "responsibility" is very significant. You have to break it in two: *response* and *ability*.

You can act in two ways – one is reaction, another is response. Reaction comes out of your past conditionings; it is mechanical. Response comes out of your presence, awareness, consciousness; it is non-mechanical. And the ability to respond is one of the greatest principles of growth. You are not following any order, any commandment, you are simply following your awareness. You are functioning like a mirror, reflecting the situation and responding to it – not out of your memory, from past experiences of similar situations; not repeating your reactions but acting fresh, new, in this very moment. Neither is the situation old, nor is your response – both are new. This ability is one of the qualities of the rebel.

Renouncing the world, escaping to the forest and the mountains, you are simply escaping from a learning situation. In a cave in the Himalayas you won't have any responsibility, but remember, without responsibility you cannot grow; your consciousness will remain stuck. For growth it needs to face, to encounter, to accept the challenges of responsibilities.

Escapists are cowards, they are not rebels – although that's what has been thought up to now, that they are rebellious spirits. They are not, they are simply cowards. They could not cope with life. They knew their weaknesses, their frailties, and they thought it was better to escape; because then you will never have to face your weakness, your frailty, you will never come to know any challenge. But without challenges how are you going to grow?

No, the rebel cannot renounce the world and the society, but he certainly renounces many other things. He renounces the so-called morality imposed upon him by the society; he renounces the so-called values imposed by the society; he renounces the knowledge given by the society. He does not renounce the society as such, but he renounces everything that the society has given to him. This is true renunciation.

The rebel lives in the society, fighting, struggling. To remain in the crowd and not to be obedient to the crowd but to be obedient to one's own conscience, is a tremendous opportunity for growth. It makes you bring out your best; it gives you a dignity.

A rebel is a fighter, a warrior. But how can you be a warrior in a cave in the Himalayas? With whom are you going to fight? The rebel remains in the society, but he is no longer part of the society – that is his renunciation and that is his rebelliousness. He is not stubborn, he is not adamant, he is not an egoist; he does not just go on fighting blindly.

If he finds something is right he obeys it, but he obeys his own feeling of rightness, not the commandment given by others. And if he sees that it is not right he disobeys it, whatsoever the cost may be. He may accept a crucifixion, but he will not accept any spiritual slavery.

The situation of the rebel is tremendously exciting: each moment he is faced with problems because the society has a fixed mode, a fixed pattern, fixed ideals. And the rebel cannot go with those fixed ideals – he has to follow his own still small voice. If his heart is saying no, there is no way, no power, to force him to say yes. You can kill him, but you cannot destroy his rebellious spirit.

His renunciation is far greater than the renunciation of Gautam Buddha, Mahavira and millions of others – they simply renounced the society, escaped into the forest, into the mountains. It was an easier way, but very dangerous because it goes against your growth.

The rebel renounces the society and still remains in it, fighting moment to moment. In this way he not only grows, he also allows the society to learn that there are many things which are not right, but have been thought to be right. There are many things which are immoral but have been thought moral; there are many things which have been thought very wise, but they are really *other*wise.

For example, all the societies of the world have praised virginity in women. It is a universally accepted ideal that the woman should remain a virgin before marriage. Sometimes there is a small, thin barrier of skin in a woman's vagina and if the woman makes love to somebody, that small barrier prevents the sperm from going to the egg.

The first thing the man is interested to know about is the small barrier, whether it is intact or not. If it is not intact then the girl is not a virgin. Sometimes riding on a horse or climbing a tree or in an accident, that small barrier can be broken, can have holes, although the girl is a virgin.

In the Middle Ages it was impossible to get a husband for her, so there were doctors who used to make an artificial skin barrier and fix it so that the woman looked virgin, whether she was virgin or not. Stupidity has no limits.

In fact, virginity should not be a part of a truly understanding society. Virginity means the woman remains unaware of what she is going to face after marriage. A more compassionate society will allow boys and girls to know sex before they get married so they know exactly what they are going for, whether they want to go for it or not. And a woman should be allowed to know as many people before marriage as possible – and the same applies to the man – because before deciding on a right partner, the only way to know is to have experiences with many partners, different types of people.

But ignorance has been propounded in the name of virginity, in the name of morality.

Ignorance cannot be supported on any grounds. If in the world married people are so miserable, one of the major reasons is that they were not allowed to know many women, many men, before their marriage; otherwise they would have chosen, with more understanding, the right person who fits harmoniously with them.

Astrologers are consulted – as if the stars are worried about whom you get married to, as if the stars are at all interested in you! Palmists are consulted, as if there are lines on your hand which can give indications for a right partner. Birth charts are consulted…all these things are absolutely irrelevant. When you were born and when the woman was born has no relationship to the life that you are going to live. But these were rationalizations. Man was trying to console himself that he has been trying every possible way to find the right partner.

There is only one way to find the right partner: that is, allow young boys and young girls to mix with as many partners as possible, so they can know the differences between women, the differences between men. Then they can come to know with whom they are polar opposites, with whom they are just lukewarm, with whom they are passionately in a harmony. Except that, there is no way of finding the right partner.

A person of rebellious spirit will have to be aware about every ideal, howsoever ancient, and will respond according to his awareness and understanding – not according to the conditioning of the society. That is true renunciation.

Lao Tzu, an authentic rebel – more authentic than Gautam Buddha and Mahavira, because he remained in the world and fought in the world – lived according to his own light, struggling, not escaping. He became so wise that the emperor invited him to become his prime minister. He simply refused. He said, "It won't work because it is improbable that we can come to the same conclusions about things. You live according to the ideals your forefathers have given to you; I live according to my own conscience." But the emperor was insistent; he could not see that there was any problem.

The very first day in his court a thief was brought in; he had been caught red-handed, stealing from the richest man in the capital – and he confessed that he was stealing. Lao Tzu gave six months in jail to both the rich man and the thief. The rich man said, "What? I have been robbed, I am a victim and I am being punished? Are you mad or something? There is no precedent in history that a man whose money has been stolen should be punished."

Lao Tzu said, "In fact, you should be given a longer term in jail than the thief – I am being much too compassionate – because you have gathered all the money of the city. Do you think money showers from the sky? Who has made these people so poor that they have to become thieves? You are responsible.

"And this will be my judgment in every case of stealing; both persons will go to jail. Your crime is far deeper, his crime is nothing. He is poor and you are responsible for it. And if he was stealing a little bit of money from your treasures, it was not much of a crime. That money belongs to many of the poor people from whom you got it. You went on becoming richer and richer and many more people went on becoming poorer and poorer."

The rich man thought, "This man seems to be crazy, utterly crazy." He said, "I want one chance to see the emperor." He was so rich that even the emperor used to borrow money from him. He told the emperor what had happened. He said to him, "If you don't remove this man from the court you will be behind bars just like me – because from where have you got all your treasures? If I am a criminal, you are a far bigger criminal."

The emperor saw the logic of the situation. He told Lao Tzu, "Perhaps you were right that it will be difficult for us to come to the same conclusions. You are relieved from your services."

This man was a rebel; he lived in the society, he struggled in the society. A rebellious mind can only think the way he thought. He was not reacting – otherwise there were precedents and law books. He was not looking in the law books and the precedents; he was looking inside his own self, watching the situation. Why are so many people poor? Who is responsible for it? Certainly those who have become too rich are the real criminals.

A rebel will renounce ideals, morals, religions, philosophies, rituals and superstitions of the society, but not the society itself. He is not a coward, he is a warrior. He has to fight his way and he has to make paths for other rebels to follow.

As far as the world is concerned...and the world and the society are not the same thing. In the past, the so-called religious people have renounced the society and the world, both. The rebel will fight against the society, renounce its ideals, and he will love the world – because the world, the existence, is our very source of life. To renounce it is to be anti-life. But all religions have been anti-life, life-negative.

The rebel should be life-affirmative. He will bring in all those values which make the world more beautiful, more lovable, which make the world more rich. It is our world – we are part of it, it is part of us – how can we renounce it? Where can we go to renounce it? The world is in the Himalayan cave as much as it is here in the marketplace.

The world has to be nourished because it is nourishing you. The world has to be respected because it is your very source of life. All the juice that flows in you, all the joys and celebrations that happen to you, come from existence itself. Rather than running away from it, you should dive deeper into it; you should send your roots to deeper sources of life and love and laughter. You should dance and celebrate.

Your celebration will bring you closer to existence, because existence is in constant celebration. Your joy, your blissfulness, your silence, will bring the silences of the stars and the sky; your peace with existence will open the doors of all the mysteries it contains. There is no other way to become enlightened.

The world has not to be condemned, it has to be respected. The rebel will honor existence, he will have immense reverence for life in whatsoever form it exists – for men, for women, for trees, for mountains, for stars. In whatever form life exists, the rebel will have a deep reverence. That will be his gratitude, that will be his prayer, that will be his religion, that will be his revolution.

To be a rebel is the beginning of a totally new kind of life, a totally new style of life; it is the beginning of a new humanity, of a new man.

I would like the whole world to be rebellious, because only in that rebelliousness will we blossom to our full potential, will we release our fragrances. We will not be repressed individuals, as man has remained for centuries…the most repressed animal. Even birds are far more free, far more natural, far more in tune with nature.

When the sun rises, it does not knock on every tree, "Wake up, the night is over." It does not go to every nest of birds, "Start singing, it is time for song." No, just as the sun rises, the flowers start opening on their own accord. And the birds start singing – not by an order from above, but from an intrinsic inevitability, from a joy, from a blissfulness.

Once I used to be a professor in a Sanskrit college. Since there were no professors' quarters immediately available and I was alone, they made arrangements for me to live in the hostel with the students. It was a Sanskrit college, following the old traditional way: each morning every student had to wake up at four o'clock, had to take a cold shower and line up by five for prayer.

For many years I used to wake up on my own in the darkness of the very early morning…and they were not even aware that I had come as a professor, because I had not started teaching yet.

It was a mistake on the part of the government to send me to that college, because I had no qualifications to teach Sanskrit. It took six months for the government to correct their mistake. Bureaucracy moves slowest, just as light moves fastest. They are the two polar opposites: light and bureaucracy.

So I had no business there and the students had no idea that I was a professor…and instead of prayer they were all abusing God, abusing the principal, abusing the whole ritual; in the cold of winter taking a cold shower – it was absolutely compulsory.

I heard this situation. I said, "This is strange…instead of being in prayer, they are doing just the opposite. Perhaps these six years in this college will be enough for them: they will never pray again in their whole lives. They will never wake up early, never again. These six years of torture will be enough of an experience."

I told the principal, "It is not right to make prayer compulsory. Prayer cannot be made compulsory; love cannot be made compulsory."

He said, "No, it is not a question of compulsion. Even if I remove the order that it is compulsory, they will still pray."

I said, "You try it "

He removed the order. Except for me, nobody woke up at four o'clock. I went and knocked on the principal's door at four o'clock. He himself was asleep – he was always asleep, he never participated in the prayer himself. I said, "Now come on and see; not a single student out of five hundred has woken up, and not a single student is praying."

The birds do not sing out of compulsion. This cuckoo is not singing because of any presidential order, because of an emergency – it is simply rejoicing with the sun, with the trees. Existence is a constant celebration. The flowers have opened their petals not because of any order – it is not a duty. It is a response – a response to the sun, a respect, a prayer, a gratitude.

A rebel lives naturally, responds naturally, becomes at home and at ease with existence. He is an existential being. That defines the rebel correctly: the existential being. Existence is his temple, existence is his holy scripture, existence is his whole philosophy. He is not an existentialist, he is existential; it is his experience.

CHAPTER 4

Understanding What Divides Us: Religion, Politics and Superstition

If religions disappear from the world, then many idiotic things will disappear with them. They are against birth control, although they know perfectly well that Jesus is the only begotten son of God – God created only one son in the whole of eternity. He must be practicing birth control; otherwise why only one son? – at least one daughter as well. But the religions are against birth control, they are against abortion, without any feeling for the danger of bringing about such over-population that the world will kill itself.

That type of death will be very cruel because it does not come immediately; when a person dies because of hunger, it takes months of torture and suffering. A healthy man can live without food for three months; then he will die. A healthy man has a reservoir of energy in his body, which is for emergency purposes. But even the poorest man, the sickest, will take a few days or a few weeks to die. Those few weeks of hunger are going to be absolute hell. But religions are concerned with creating more children because more children means more power – more votes, and more fodder for your cannons in war.

For twenty to thirty years absolute birth control should be practiced. It is not a question of democracy, because it is a choice between life and death. If the whole world is going to die, what are you going to do with your democracy? Democracy will be the rule then – "for the graves, of the graves, by the graves" – because the people will have disappeared.

Religions carry superstitions of all kinds which are hindering your intelligence, your vision, your possibility of creating a new man in the world.

One thing is certain – the old type of humanity is going to die. If we can make the people of the world understand, then a new kind of man can survive.

He will be a citizen of the world – no nations. He will be religious but there will be no religion. He will be scientific but not destructive; his whole science will be devoted to creation. He will be pious, compassionate, loving – but not celibate! That is a kind of lunacy. A celibate is a lunatic.

The new man will stop all kinds of experiments that are increasing the heat of the atmosphere around the earth, because the priority is life, not your experiments. The new man will not send rockets to create holes from which death rays can enter into our atmosphere; there is no need at all. And if the need arises, then you should also be prepared to close those holes – the moment the rocket goes out, the hole is closed; the moment the rocket comes in, the hole is closed.

That is the only way to avoid the seas bringing back the old story of the flood in which everything was destroyed…and now even Noah's Ark will not help, because the flood will never recede.

A new man without any burden of the past, more meditative, more silent, more loving…all the universities, rather than wasting their time on superficial subjects, should devote time to creating more consciousness in human beings. But football seems to be more important. It is one of the most idiotic games…and millions of people go mad when there is a football match.

I know one of my friends – he is a professor – he takes leave when there is a football match. If he cannot go to the match itself, then he sits in front of his television set. I was staying with him, he lives in Amritsar. Television came first to Pakistan, because Pakistan is an ally of

America; it came to India almost twenty years afterwards. But Amritsar is only fifteen miles away from Pakistan, so they were enjoying Pakistani programs on television, even when in India there was no television. I was staying with that friend, and I got fed up sitting in the room, because watching a football match...it is so idiotic! Millions of people are going mad, as if something very crucial is involved. And because the team that he was identified with was defeated, he threw his television set on the floor, he was so angry.

I said, "You must be an idiot! That I knew from the very beginning, but what is the crime of the poor television set?"

He said, "I became so enraged. It is absolutely unjust."

But I said, "It may be unjust or just, the television set is not involved in it."

He said, "It is not a question of the television set. I was so angry, I wanted to destroy something."

In a California university, for a year they did a research study to see what happens whenever there is a boxing match – which is the ugliest thing you can conceive of, people hitting on each other's noses. Boxing proves Charles Darwin is right: man has come from animals and still has animal instincts in him. The study of the California university is very significant: they found that whenever there is a boxing match, crime rates go fourteen percent higher immediately, and they remain at that level for at least a week – fourteen percent higher! Just watching people hitting each other, their own animal becomes alive – more murders, more rape, more suicides. It takes seven days for them to calm down, back to their normal criminality. Still, boxing is not banned.

And a new phenomenon has started, and that is small children are committing crimes, which has never happened before – thirteen-year-old boys, twelve-year-old boys trying to rape girls; ten-year-old boys, nine-year-old boys murdering, assassinating; seven-year-olds, eight-year-olds taking drugs. Now drugs are not just a problem with adult people, but also for primary school children.

But nobody seems to be concerned about why this is happening. It can be prevented. People use drugs because without drugs they are so much in anguish and anxiety drugs calm down their minds for a few hours. But again the problems are back. Unless meditation becomes an absolute in every educational institution, drugs cannot be prohibited. You can prohibit them, but they go underground. Man has to be taught some other ways of becoming calm and quiet and blissful, then there is no need for all these things.

A fourteen-year-old boy committing rape simply shows that you have to change your attitudes about sex. Boys and girls should be raised in hostels together; they should be allowed to make love with no inhibition. Up to a certain age there is no problem, because the girls are not going to get pregnant, so it is simply a game, a joyful game they can enjoy. But rape is a crime – and you are responsible for it.

By the time the girls are of the age that they can become pregnant, the pill should be available in every institution. And now there are pills available for men also; either the girl can take it or the boy can take it. In the past it used to happen sometimes that you had not taken the pill, and suddenly you met your lover – and everybody always thinks, "This is not going to happen to me...." But now they have found a pill that can be taken after lovemaking. It is more secure.

Things should be thought about in a scientific way, not in a superstitious way; then there is a possibility of man's future.

If we take a serious step against all the dangers that are facing humanity, there is a possibility of a new man, of a better man, of a natural man, of a healthier man, of a more religious man in the future...a world without wars, without nations, without religions...a world peaceful, loving...a world in search of truth, of bliss, of ecstasy.

But if these problems are not solved immediately, there is no future possible.

✼

Our problems are international but our solutions are national. No one nation is able to solve them. I take it as a great challenge and as a great opportunity.

Nations should be collapsed into one world government. It was tried by the League of Nations before the Second World War, but it could not succeed. It simply remained a debating club. The Second World War destroyed the very credibility of the League of Nations. But the necessity was still there; therefore they had to create the United Nations. But the UN is as much a failure as the League of Nations was.

It is still a debating club because it has no power. It cannot implement anything, it is just a formal club.

I would like a world government. All nations should surrender their armies, their arms to the world government. Certainly if there is a world government, neither armies are needed, nor arms. With whom are you going to have a war? To find the closest neighbor amongst the planets for some kind of war seems almost impossible.

Nations have become out of date, but they go on existing – and they are the greatest problem. Looking at the world as a bird sees it, a strange feeling arises: we have everything else that we need, it is just that we need one humanity.

India has so much coal; Russia has no coal at all, but they have an overproduction of wheat. Half the population of India goes on starving; it needs wheat, it certainly cannot eat coal. But in the Soviet Union in the time of Stalin they were burning wheat in their railway trains instead of coal. They didn't have coal but they had an abundance of crops. It was easy for them to burn the wheat, but they didn't realize that they were really burning millions of people, who were dying because they didn't have anything to eat.

Problems are worldwide. Solutions have also to be worldwide. And it is absolutely clear that there are things that are not needed in one place, and somewhere else the very life depends on them. A world government means looking at the whole situation of this globe and shifting things where they are needed. It is one humanity.

In Ethiopia one thousand people per day were dying and in Europe and America they were drowning billions of dollars worth of food in the ocean, because they have better technology for production. Anybody looking from the outside will think that humanity is insane. Thousands of people are dying and mountains of butter and other foodstuff is being drowned in the ocean?

Europe and America both have millions of people who cannot afford enough food. So it is not even a question of giving to somebody else, it is a question of giving to its own people! But the problem becomes complicated, because if you start giving free food to millions of people, then others will start asking, "Why should we pay for our food?" Then the prices of things will go down. With the prices going down, the farmers will not be interested anymore in producing – what is the point? Afraid of disturbing the economy, millions of people die on the streets while we go on drowning the surplus food in the ocean.

Not only that, millions of people are sick and dying in American hospitals, particularly, from diseases caused by overeating. They cannot be allowed to stay at home, because in the home it is very difficult to protect the fridge from those people! They are dying because they eat too much, and on the street there are people dying because they have nothing to eat.

But a bird's eye view is needed to look at the world, all over, as one unit. Our problems have brought us to a situation where either we will have to commit suicide or we will have to transform man, his old traditions, his conditionings. Those conditionings and those educational systems, those religions that man has followed up to now, have contributed to this crisis. This global crisis is the ultimate outcome of all our cultures, all our philosophies, all our religions. They all have contributed to it – in strange ways, because nobody ever thought of the whole; everybody was looking at a small piece, not bothering about the whole. Everybody has taken a certain portion of life, ignoring the remaining parts which are essentially joined with it. Instead, people keep on behaving in ways that will destroy the whole earth. And those who are doing these things are doing them behind great names: nations, religions, political ideologies, communism.

It seems man exists for all these kinds of things – communism, democracy, socialism, fascism. The reality should be that everything should exist for man, and if it goes against man it should not exist at all. The whole past of humanity is full of stupid ideologies for which people have been crusading, killing, murdering, burning living people. We have to drop all this insanity.

So first the nations should go, if the world is to survive; second, the religions should go. One humanity is enough – there is no need of India and England and Germany. And one religiousness is enough: meditation, truth, love, authenticity, sincerity, which do not need any name – Hindu, Christian, Mohammedan…just one religiousness, a quality, not something organized. The moment organization comes in there is going to be violence, because there will be other organizations in conflict. We need a world of individuals without any organizations. Yes, people who have similar feelings, similar joys, rejoicings, can have gatherings. But there should not be any organizations, hierarchies, bureaucracies.

First nations, second religions, and third, a science completely devoted to better life, to more life, to better intelligence, to more creativity – not to create more war, not to be destructive. If these three things are possible, the whole humanity can be saved from being destroyed by its own leaders – religious, political, social.

Crisis in a way is good because it is going to force people to choose. Do you want to die or do you want to live a new life? Die to the past, drop all that has been given as heritage from the past and start fresh, as if you have descended on this earth for the first time. And then start working with nature not as an enemy but as a friend, and ecology will soon be functioning again as an organic unity.

The damage can be repaired; it is not difficult to make the earth more green. If many trees have been cut, many more trees can be planted. And with scientific help they can grow faster, they can have better foliage. Different kinds of barriers can be created in the rivers so that they don't flood poor countries like Bangladesh. The same water can create much more electricity and help thousands of villages to have light in the night, to have warmth in the cold winters.

It is a simple thing. All problems are simple, but the basic foundation is the trouble. Those three things will try in every way not to disappear, even at the cost of the whole world disappearing. They will be ready for this disappearance, but they will not be ready to declare, "We surrender to a world organization all our arms, all our armies."

The function of nations will remain only simple: railway lines, post offices, a small police force to take care of internal affairs. But there is no need of armies. Millions of people are involved in armies, which are useless. They can be put to creative arts, to farming, to gardening. And they are trained people, they can do jobs which no other people can do. An army can make a bridge so quickly – that is its training – it can create more houses for people.

Science is capable now, if it is no longer engaged only in war and creating more war material, to create so much food that even more people can live happily on this earth than exist today. Billions and billions of people can live joyously without hunger, without suffering from diseases. But science should be released from the hands of nations, which are forcing their scientists to create more weapons and destructive technology. Scientists are functioning almost like prisoners.

I want it to be known to the whole world: if you anot ready to be one, be ready to disappear from this planet. But I hope there are intelligent people who would like to survive, who would like this beautiful planet to grow more beautiful, this humanity to grow more intelligent. I am afraid perhaps the whole of humanity is not even aware of the danger that is coming closer every moment.

And finally we need, with these three fundamental changes, a great respect for creative people of any dimension. We should learn how to transform our energies so that they are not repressed, so they are expressed in your love, in your laughter, in your joy. This earth is more than a paradise, you don't have to go anywhere. Paradise is not something that has to be achieved, it is something that has to be created. It depends on us.

This crisis gives a chance for courageous people to disconnect themselves from the past and start living in a new way – not modified, not continuous with the past, not better than the past, but absolutely new.

Find ways to relate in a new way. Forget marriages, start thinking how to enquire into life. Forget all your beliefs, start to meditate in search of finding exactly who you are, because by finding yourself you will have found the very essence of existence. It is immortal and eternal, and those who have found it, their bliss and their benediction is inexpressible.

We need more happy people around the earth. Nuclear weapons and destructive war machines cannot work by themselves. They are being worked by human beings, behind them are human hands. A hand that knows the beauty of a rose flower cannot drop a bomb on Hiroshima. A hand that knows the beauty of love is not the hand to keep a gun loaded with death. Just a little contemplation and you will understand what I am saying.

I am saying, spread laughter, spread love, spread life-affirmative values, grow more flowers around the earth. Everything that is beautiful, appreciate it, and everything that is inhuman, condemn it. Take this whole earth away from the hands of the politicians and the priests and you will have saved the world, and you will have changed the world into a totally new phenomenon, with a new human consciousness. And it has to be done now, because the time is very short.

Our work here is to teach people consciousness, more awareness, more love, more understanding, more joy, and spread the dance and celebration around the earth. Reduced to a single statement, I can say: if we can make humanity happier, there is not going to be any third world war.

Giovanni wants to have a ride on a bicycle so he decides to go and ask his friend Mario if he can borrow his. On the way he starts to think, "For sure, Mario will tell me to be careful with the bike, but I will tell him not to worry; then he will tell me that his sister wants to use it, but I will tell him that I will be back in time; then I know Mario will get scared and tell me it is not the time of year for riding bikes...."

Finally, Giovanni arrives at Mario's house – and he looks up to the window and shouts, "Hey, Mario! Go and fuck yourself, you and your bike!"

Hamish MacTavish has not seen his old friend, Gordon MacPherson for forty years. So when they bump into each other in the street one day, they rush to the nearest pub to celebrate.

"It will be wonderful to have a drink together after all these years," says Gordon.

"Aye, it will," says Hamish. "But don't forget, it is your round."

There is an accident on the construction site. Seamus runs over to where Paddy is lying in a heap of rubble.

"Are you dead, Paddy, after such a terrible fall?" asks Seamus.

"Yes, certainly I am," replies Paddy.

"Ah, bejabers!" says Seamus, "you are such a terrible liar, I don't know whether to believe you or not."

"That proves I am dead, you idiot," says Paddy. "If I was alive, you would not be calling me a liar to my face."

The last....

Hamish MacTavish is careering down the road in his old Ford car when a policeman pulls him over.

"Excuse me, sir," says the cop. "Would you mind blowing into this bag?"

"By all means," says Hamish. "Would you like me to play a jig or a reel?"

"No, no," says the cop. "This bag tells you how much you have been drinking."

"Oh, there is no need for that," says Hamish. "I have got one of my own at home…I married her!"

> *Why are you so much against the religions? Don't they serve an important role in providing a moral compass for people's behavior?*

I am against all organized religions, without any exception, for the simple reason that truth cannot be organized. It is not politics, it is a love affair between the individual and existence; you cannot organize it. No priests are needed, no theologians are needed, no churches are needed.

Is not the sky full of stars enough for you to appreciate and admire, and fall down on the earth in prayer and in thankfulness to existence? Are not flowers enough, trees and birds, mountains…a sunrise, a beautiful sunset? Existence surrounds you with so much beauty, and you create a small prison and call it a church. And you think going into the church is being religious?

Listening to the sermon of a man who has not realized anything – he may be a scholar, but he is not enlightened; he speaks within quotes, but he cannot speak on his own authority – is simply wasting time. Find somebody who has found the truth, and be with him. Drink his presence; look into his eyes. Feel his heart and let your heart beat in rhythm with his heart, and perhaps you may have some taste of religion. But religion cannot be organized.

Truth cannot even be expressed, what to say about organizing it? It is inexpressible. Those who have known it have talked about and about, but they have never been able to exactly say it. They talk and about in the hope that perhaps by chance you may get the knack.

It is not an art which can be taught; it is something more like a disease which can only be caught. When you are near a man who knows the truth, perhaps you may catch the disease.

All the mystics of the world, of all the ages, are agreed on one point, that truth cannot be brought down to the level of language. All the theologians are doing just the opposite. All the mystics are agreed that there is no way of organizing truth, because it is purely an individual affair. Do you have organizations for love? And love at least involves two persons; it is interpersonal.

Religion is absolutely personal. It does not involve anybody else but you.

You need not be a part of a crowd, Catholic, Protestant, Christian, Hindu, Mohammedan, Buddhist. All these crowds have destroyed the possibility of man attaining truth, because they have given a fallacious idea that you need not search: "Jesus knows – you simply believe in Jesus. Buddha knows it; simply believe in Buddha. You don't have to do anything." They have made truth so cheap that the whole world believes and lives in darkness, and lives in a thousand and one lies.

Belief in the very beginning is a lie. How can you believe that Buddha has attained truth? How can you believe that Jesus has attained truth? His contemporaries did not even believe him and you are twenty centuries away! His contemporaries only thought he was a nuisance. They did not relish his presence; on the contrary, they wanted him to be destroyed. And you say you know that he knew the truth? On what grounds?

Your belief is just a strategy to deceive yourself. You don't want to take the arduous path of seeking, searching, discovering. It is arduous, because you will have to drop many superstitions, and you will have to deprogram yourself from many conditions of the past which are preventing you from knowing the truth, from knowing yourself. No belief can help, and all religions are based on belief – that's why they are called faiths, and the religious people are called faithful.

Truth is a search, not a faith. It is an enquiry, not a belief. It is a question, a quest, and you will have to go a long way to find it. To avoid this long journey you easily become gullible. You easily become victims of anybody who is ready to exploit you. And naturally it feels cozy in a crowd. There are six hundred million Catholics; it feels cozy, and you feel that six hundred million people cannot be wrong. You may be wrong, but six hundred million people cannot be wrong. And everybody else in those six hundred million people is thinking the same. Four hundred million Hindus feel that they are right; otherwise, why should four hundred million believe in their truth? The same is true about Mohammedans, Buddhists and other religions.

The search for truth is a flight of the alone to the alone.

All these religions have made you parts of crowds, dependent on the crowds. They have taken away your individuality, they have taken away your freedom, they have taken away your intelligence. In its place they have given you bogus beliefs which mean nothing.

I am not particularly against any particular religion, I am against all religions. My standpoint is that to be religious is a personal experience. A Buddha may have known truth, but the moment Buddha dies his truth disappears like a fragrance. When a flower dies, what happens to the fragrance? It moves into the universal.

It is good that everybody has to find it again and again; otherwise truth would be such a boring thing. It is an adventure and an ecstasy – and it will remain always an adventure, because it cannot be purchased, it cannot be borrowed, it cannot be stolen, it cannot be believed. There is no other way except seeking it and finding it.

The very seeking is so beautiful. Each moment of it is such a joy, because each moment something falls, drops from your life. And we are surrounded by falsities. On each step some mask drops, and you become acquainted with your original face. And finally, when all that is false has disappeared, you become a light unto yourself, and that is the moment of religiousness.

I would love the whole world to be religious – not as part of any organized religion, but as an independent search, arising out of each individual's freedom. Then you will have an authority. Then, whether you say it or not, even your silence will be a sermon, even your gestures will have a grace. Those who are receptive will immediately feel the pull of the realized person, the magnetic force in his eyes, in his presence.

There is no need to convert anybody; every conversion is ugly. When you come across somebody who knows, you simply fall in love.

It is not a conversion, it is simply that you cannot do anything else. In spite of you, something goes on pulling you into a new direction, into a new dimension.

Basically I am for freedom of the individual for seeking the truth. Unfortunately, because of this, I have to be against organized religions. But that is not my joy, it is just the dirty work I have to do.

> *You have criticized the United Nations universal "Declaration of Human Rights" on the grounds that, while perhaps well-intentioned, it is hypocritical and fails to understand the real causes of injustice and abuses of human freedoms. What would you propose to ensure that human rights are honored in the new human community that you envision?*

The UN Declaration of Human Rights basically means that mankind still lives in many kinds of slaveries. Otherwise, there would be no need for a declaration. The very need indicates that man has been deceived for thousands of years – and he has been deceived in such a cunning way that unless you rise above humanity, you cannot see in what invisible chains you are living, in what bondage, in what invisible prisons everybody is confined.

My declaration of human rights consists of ten fundamental things.

The first is life.

Man has a right to dignity, to health; a right to grow, so that he can blossom into his ultimate flowering. This ultimate flowering is his right. He is born with the seeds, but the society does not provide him the soil, the right caring, the loving atmosphere. On the contrary, society provides a poisonous atmosphere full of anger, hatred, destructiveness, violence, war. The right to life means there should be no wars anymore. It also means that nobody should be forced into armies, forced to go to war; it should be everybody's right to refuse. But this is not the case.

Thousands of people have been sent to prisons – particularly young people, sensitive and intelligent – because they refused to go to war. Their refusal has been treated as a crime – and they were simply saying that they don't want to kill human beings!

Human beings are not things you can destroy without a second thought. They are the climax of universal evolution. To destroy them for any cause is wrong – for religion, for politics, for socialism, for fascism, it does not matter what the cause is. Man is above all causes, and man cannot be sacrificed on any altar.

It is so strange that the UN declares the fundamental rights of human beings and yet says nothing about those thousands of young people wasting their lives in prisons for the simple reason that they refused to destroy life. But the phenomenon has deep roots which have to be understood.

The right to life is possible only in a certain different atmosphere, which is not present on the earth at the moment. Animals are killed, birds are killed, sea animals are killed just for game. You don't have any reverence for life. And life is the same whether it is in human beings or in other forms. Unless man becomes aware of his violence towards animals, birds, he cannot be really alert about his own right to life. If you are not caring about others' lives, what right have you got to demand the same right for yourself?

People go hunting, killing animals unnecessarily. I was a guest in Maharaja Jamnagar's palace. He showed me hundreds of lions, deer – their heads. The whole palace was full, and he was showing them off: "These are the animals I have killed myself."

I asked him, "You look like a nice a person. What was the reason? What have these animals done against you?"

He said, "It is not a question of having a reason, or of them doing anything against me. It is just a game."

I said, "Just look at it from the other side: If a lion killed you, would that be a game? Your wife, your children, your brothers – will any one of them have the guts to say that it was a beautiful game? It will be a disaster! If you kill an animal, then it is a game; if they kill you, then it is a calamity. These double standards show your dishonesty, insincerity."

He said, "I have never thought about it."

But most of humanity is non-vegetarian; they are all eating other life forms. There is no reverence for life as such. Unless we create an atmosphere of reverence for life, man cannot realize the goal of getting his fundamental right to life.

Secondly, because the UN also declares life to be a fundamental right for man, it is being misused. The pope, Mother Teresa, and their tribe are using it for teaching people against birth control, against abortion, against the pill. Man's mind is so cunning! It was a question of human rights, and they are taking advantage of it. They are saying you cannot use birth control methods because they go against life; the unborn child also has the same right as you have. So some line has to be drawn, because at what point does life exist?

To me, the pill does not destroy human rights; in fact it prepares the ground for it. If the earth is too overcrowded, millions of people will die of starvation; there will be wars. And the way the crowd is exploding it can lead humanity into a very inhuman situation.

In Bengal, there was a great famine in which mothers ate their own dead children. People sold their dying children just for one rupee, two rupees. And do you think the persons who were purchasing them were purchasing human beings? No, they were purchasing food. The pope and Mother Teresa will be responsible for all this.

The pill simply does not allow the child to be formed in the mother's womb, so the question of human rights does not arise. And science has found a pill for men too. It is not necessary that the woman should take the pill, the man can take it. The child is not formed in any way; hence, this fundamental right is inapplicable in that case. But these religious people – the *shankaracharyas* in India, the ayatollahs in Iran…all over the world, all religions are against birth control. And they are the only methods which can prevent man from falling into a barbarous state.

I am absolutely in favor of birth control methods. A child should be recognized as a human being when he is born – and then too, I have some reservations. If a child is born blind, if a child is born crippled, if a child is born deaf, dumb, and we cannot do anything to help the child… Just because life should not be destroyed, this child will have to suffer because of your stupid idea – for seventy years, eighty years. Why create unnecessary suffering? If the parents are willing, the child should be put to eternal sleep. And there is no problem in it. Only the body goes back into its basic elements; the soul will fly into another womb. Nothing is destroyed. If you really love the child, you will not want him to live a seventy-year-long life in misery, suffering, sickness, old age. So even if a child is born, if he is not medically capable of enjoying life fully then it is better that he goes to eternal sleep and is born somewhere else with a better body.

The right to life is a complex thing. Nobody is entitled to kill anyone, either, in the name of religion. Millions of people have been killed in the name of religions, in the service of God. No one should be killed in the name of politics. Again, the same has happened. Joseph Stalin alone killed a million of his own people, while he was in power. Adolf Hitler killed six million people. And thousands of wars have happened.

It seems that on this earth we are doing only one thing: reproducing children because soldiers are needed, reproducing children because wars are needed. Even to increase the population, Mohammed said that every Mohammedan can marry four women or even more. He himself married nine women. And the reason is war, destruction of life. It is not out of love for nine women that he has married them, it is simple arithmetic. If a man marries nine women, he can produce nine children in one year. If nine women marry one man, this is okay – but with nine men marrying one woman she may not be able even to produce one child. They will mess up the whole thing. Most probably they will kill the woman!

It seems that the human being is nothing but a necessary instrument for more destruction, more wars.

The population has to be reduced if man wants to have his dignity, honor, his right to live – not just to drag, but to dance. When I say life is a fundamental right, I mean a life of songs and dances, a life of joy and blessings.

My second consideration is for love.

Love should be accepted as one of the most fundamental human rights, and all societies have destroyed it. They have destroyed it by creating marriage. Marriage is a false substitute for love.

In the past, even small children were married. They had no idea what love is, what marriage is. And why were small children married? For a simple reason: before they become young adults, before love arises in their hearts the doors have to be closed. Because once love takes possession of their hearts then it will become very difficult....

No child marriage is human. A man or a woman should be allowed to choose their partners and to change their partners whenever they feel. The government has no business in it, the society has nothing to do with it. It is two individuals' personal affair. The privacy of it is sacred. If two people want to live together, they don't need any permission from any priest or any government, they need the permission of their hearts. And the day they feel that the time has come to part, again they don't need anybody's permission. They can part as friends, with beautiful memories of their loving days.

Love should be the only way for men and women to live together. No other ritual is needed.

The only problem in the past was what would happen to the children; that was the argument for marriage. There are other alternatives, far better. Children should be accepted not as their parents' property – they belong to the whole humanity. From the very beginning it should be made clear to them: "The whole of humanity is going to protect you, is going to be your shelter. We may be together – we will look after you. We may not be together; still we look after you. You are our blood, our bones, our souls."

In fact, this possession by the parents of the children is one of the most dangerous things that humanity goes on perpetuating. This is the root of the idea of possessiveness. You should not possess your children. You can love them, you can bless them, but you cannot possess them. They belong to the whole of humanity. They come from beyond; you have been just a passage. Don't think of yourself as more than that. Whatever you can do, do.

Every community, every village should take care of the children. Once the commune starts taking care of the children, marriage becomes absolutely obsolete. And marriage is destroying your basic right to love.

If man's love is free, there will not be blacks and whites, and there will not be these ugly discriminations, because love knows no boundaries. You can fall in love with a black man, you can fall in love with a white man. Love knows no religious scriptures. It knows only the heartbeat, and it knows it with absolute certainty. Once love is free, it will prepare the ground for other fundamental rights.

In fact, if you ask the scientists, people falling in love should be as different as possible. Then they will give birth to better children, more intelligent, stronger. We know it now; we are trying it all over the world as far as animals are concerned. Crossbreeding has given us better cows, better horses, better dogs. But man is strange. You know the secret, but you are not bettering yourself.

There should be no boundaries insisting that a Hindu should marry only a Hindu, or a brahmin should only marry a brahmin. In fact, the rule should be that the Indian should never marry an Indian. The whole world is there; find your spouse far away, beyond the seven seas, and then you will have children who are more beautiful, healthier, living longer, far more intelligent, geniuses. Man has to learn cross-breeding, but that is possible only if marriage disappears and love is given absolute respect. Right now it is condemned.

The third most fundamental right…because these are the three most important things in life: life, love, and death. Everybody should be given the fundamental right that after a certain age, when he has lived enough and does not want to go on dragging unnecessarily… Because tomorrow will be again just a repetition; he has lost all curiosity about tomorrow. He has every right to leave the body. It is his fundamental right. It is his life; if he does not want to continue, nobody should prevent him. In fact, every hospital should have a special ward where people who want to die can enter a month before, can relax, enjoy all the things that they have been thinking about their whole life but could not manage – the music, the literature, if they wanted to paint or sculpt....

And the doctors should take care to teach them how to relax. Up to now, death has been almost ugly. Man has been a victim, but it is our fault. Death can be made a celebration; you just have to learn how to welcome it, relaxed and peaceful. And in one month's time, friends can come to see the person and meet together. Every hospital should have special facilities – more facilities for those who are going to die than for those who are going to live. Let them live for one month at least like emperors, so they can leave life with no grudge, with no complaint but only with deep gratitude, thankfulness.

Between these three comes the fourth: the search for truth.

Nobody should be conditioned from childhood about any religion, any philosophy, any theology, because you are destroying his freedom of search. Help him to be strong enough. Help him to be strong enough to doubt, to be skeptical about all that is believed all around him. Help him never to believe but to insist on knowing. And whatever it takes, however long it takes, to go for the pilgrimage alone, on his own, because there is no other way to find the truth.

All others – who think they are Christians, or they are Jews, or they are Hindus, or they are Mohammedans – these are all believers. They don't know. Belief is pure poison.

Knowing is coming to a flowering.

The search for truth…you should not teach anybody what truth is because it cannot be taught. You should help the person to inquire. Inquiry is difficult; belief is cheap. But truth is not cheap; truth is the most valuable thing in the world. You cannot get it from others, you will have to find it yourself.

And the miracle is, the moment you decide that "I will not fall victim to any belief," you have already traveled half the way toward truth. If your determination is total, you need not go to truth, truth will come to you. You just have to be silent enough to receive it. You have to become a host so that truth can become a guest in your heart.

Right now the whole world is living in beliefs. That's why there is no shine in the eyes, no grace in people's gestures, no strength, no authority in their words. Belief is bogus; it is making castles of sand. A little breeze and your great castle will be destroyed.

Truth is eternal, and to find it means you also become part of eternity.

Fifth: to find the truth, all education systems from the kindergarten to the universities will create a certain atmosphere for meditation. Meditation does not belong to any religion, and meditation is not a belief. It is a pure science of the inner. Learning to be silent, learning to be watchful, learning to be a witness; learning that you are not the mind, but something beyond – the consciousness – will prepare you to receive truth.

And it is truth that has been called "god" by many people, by others, "nirvana." By others, other names have been given to it but it is a nameless silence, serenity, peace. The peace is so deep that you disappear; and the moment you disappear you have entered the temple of the divine.

But people are wasting almost one-third of their lives in schools, colleges, and universities, not knowing anything about silence, not knowing anything about relaxation, not knowing anything about themselves. They know about the whole world – it is very strange that they have forgotten only themselves. But it seems there is some reason....

In India there is an ancient story. Ten blind men pass through a stream. The current is very forceful, so they hold hands. Reaching the other side, somebody suggests, "We should count ourselves. The current was so strong and we cannot see – somebody may have gone with the river."

So they count. Strangely enough, the counting always stops at nine. Everybody tries, but it is always nine. One man sitting on the bank of the river starts laughing – it is hilarious! And those ten blind people are sitting there crying, tears in their eyes because they have lost one of their friends. The man comes to them and he says, "What is the matter?"

They explain the situation. He says, "You all stand up in a line. I will hit the first person – he has to say 'one.' I will hit the second person – he has to say 'two,' because I will hit twice. I will hit the third person three times; he has to say 'three.'"

Strangely enough, he finds the tenth man who was lost. They all thank him, they touch his feet; they say, "You are a god to us. We were thinking we had lost one of our friends. But please, can you tell us…we were also counting; all of us tried, and the tenth was not here. How has he appeared suddenly?"

The man says, "That is an ancient mystery which you will not understand. You just go on your way."

What is the ancient mystery in it? One tends to forget oneself. In fact, one lives his whole life without remembering himself. He sees everybody else, he knows everybody else; he just forgets himself.

Meditation is the only method in which you will start counting from yourself: "one."

And because it is not part of any religion, there is no problem – it should be all over the world, in every school, in every college, in every university. Anybody who comes home from the university should come with a deep, meditative being, with an aura of meditation around him. Otherwise, what he is bringing is all rubbish, crap. Geography he knows, he knows where Timbuktu is, he knows where Constantinople is – and he does not know where he is himself!

The first thing in life is to know who you are, where you are. Then everything in your life starts settling, moving in the right direction.

The sixth: freedom in all dimensions.

We are not even as free as birds and animals. No bird goes to the passport office. Any moment he can fly from India into Pakistan with no entry visa. Strange that only man remains confined in nations, in boundaries. Because the nation is big, you tend to forget that you are imprisoned. You cannot get out of it, others cannot get into it. It is a big prison, and the whole earth is full of big prisons.

Freedom in all dimensions means that man, wherever he is born, is part of one humanity.

Nations should dissolve, religions should dissolve, because they are all creating bondages – and sometimes hilarious bondages.

I was in a city, Devas. For twenty years the Jaina temple there has not opened. There are three locks on the temple: one lock from the *Digambaras*, one of the sects of Jainism, one from another sect, *Svetambaras*, and the third from the police. When I saw it, I asked, "What is the matter?" I was just passing by and I saw three locks – big locks, bigger than you may have ever seen – and I came to know the story.

There is only one Jaina temple in Devas, and this was the temple. Jainas are few in the city; they didn't have enough money to make two temples, so they made one temple and divided the time. Up to twelve o'clock in the morning, Digambaras could worship, and after twelve, Svetambaras could worship…but there was a fight every day.

The differences between Svetambaras and Digambaras are not very great – so childish and so stupid. Digambaras worship Mahavira with closed eyes and Svetambaras worship Mahavira with open eyes. This is the only basic difference.

Now a marble statue…either you can make the eyes closed or you can make the eyes open…unless you create some mechanism, some switch so he opens and closes his eyes depending on whether you switch it on or switch it off. But that kind of technology did not exist; otherwise it would not be difficult. You can find it in toys – a beautiful doll, you lie her down and she closes her eyes. You put her back on her feet and she opens her eyes. Something could have been arranged.

And in fact they had arranged something – primitive, but they had arranged it. When Svetambaras worshipped the statue, which has closed eyes, they put false eyes on top. They just glue them on. That is simple, non-technical; not much technology is needed.

But every day the problem was there: at the time of twelve, exactly twelve, the Svetambaras would be waiting. One minute more…and the Digambaras would be worshipping knowingly a little longer. So the Svetambaras would come into the temple and start putting their eyes on the statue, and the fight would start.

It happened so many times that finally the police locked the temple and said to them, "Go to the court and get a decision." The case goes on – how can the court decide whether Mahavira used to meditate with closed eyes or with open eyes? The reality is that he used to meditate with half open eyes.

No child should be given any idea by the parents what life is all about – no theology, no philosophy, no politics. He should be made as intelligent and sharp as possible, so when he comes of age he can go in search. And it is a lifelong search. People today get their religion when they are born. In fact, if you can get your religion when you die, you have found it early. It is such a precious treasure, but it is possible only out of freedom – and freedom in all dimensions, not only in religion.

There should be no nations, no national boundaries. There should be no religions. A human being should be taken as a human being. Why confine yourself with so many adjectives? Right now you are not free in any way.

I was going to college. My parents wanted me to go to science college or to medical college. I said, "Am I going or are you going?"

They said, "Of course you are going; why should we be going?"

"Then," I said, "leave it to me."

They said, "We can leave it to you, but then remember: we will not support you financially."

I said, "That's understood." I left my home without a single rupee. I traveled in the train to the university without a ticket. I had to go to the ticket checker and tell him: "This is the situation. Can you allow me to travel without a ticket?"

He said, "This is the first time in my life that somebody has come to ask me! People hide, people deceive me, cheat me. Certainly I will take you, and at the university station I will be at the gate so nobody bothers you."

I went directly to the vice-chancellor and told him the whole story. And I told him, "I want to study philosophy, but it seems there is no freedom even to choose what I want to study. So you have to give me all the scholarships possible, because I will not be getting any financial help. Otherwise I will study philosophy, fasting…even if I die."

He said, "No! Don't do that, because then the blame will be on me. I will give you all the scholarships."

From the very childhood we go on crippling, cutting freedoms; we try to make a child according to our desires.

I was talking to a Christian missionary and he said, "God made man in his own image."

I said, "That is the foundation of all slavery. Why should God make man in his own image? Who is he? – and to give his own image to man means he has destroyed man from the very beginning." And that is what every father is doing.

Man's basic right is to be himself.

And in an authentic human society, everybody should be allowed to be himself – even if he chooses just to be a flute player, and he will not become the richest man in the world but will be a beggar on the streets. Still I say freedom is so valuable… You may not be the president of the country, you may be just a beggar playing the flute in the streets. But you are yourself, and there is such deep contentment, fulfillment, that unless you know it you have missed the train.

Seventh: one earth, one humanity.

I don't see any reason at all why there should be so many nations. Why should there be so many lines on the map? And they are only on the map, remember. They are not on the earth; neither are they in the sky. The map is man-made. Existence has not created this earth in fragments.

I am reminded of one of my teachers. He was a very loving human being, and he had his own methods of teaching. He was a kind of rebel.

One day he came with a few pieces of cardboard, placed them on the table, and said to us all, "Look, this is the map of the world, but I have cut it into pieces and I have mixed them up. Now anybody who is confident that he can put them in their right places and make the world map should come up."

One tried, failed; another tried, failed. I went on watching him and watching the people who were failing and why they were failing.

Watching five persons fail, I was the sixth. I went and I turned over all his cardboard pieces. He said, "What are you doing?"

I said, "You wait, I am working it out. Five people have failed but I have found the secret."

On the other side of the map was a picture of a man. I arranged the man, which was easier. On one side the man was arranged and on the other side the whole map of the world was arranged. That was the key that I had been looking for, waiting to see if I could get some clue. And when the others were arranging the pieces, I saw that there was something on the other side.

The teacher said, "You are a rascal! I was hoping you would come first, but when you didn't come I understood that you were waiting to find out the key. And you have found the right key."

The world is divided because man is divided; man is divided because the world is divided.

Start from anywhere; just let the whole of humanity be one, and the nations will disappear, the lines will disappear. It is our world – one humanity, one earth, and we can make it a paradise. Right now there is no need to describe hell. You can just look all around; it is here! Man is in such misery and suffering that there seems to be no need for another hell.

But we can change the whole situation. This earth can become a paradise. And then there will be no need for any paradise; paradise will be empty.

Eighth: uniqueness of every individual.

A very beautiful word has been misused so utterly that it is difficult to imagine, and that word is equality.

A few thinkers say human beings are equal. To honor them, the UN declares that equality is man's birthright. But nobody bothers to see that man is not equal and has never been equal. It is absolutely un-psychological.

Every person is unique. The moment you are all equal you are a crowd, your individuality has been taken away. You are no longer yourself but just a cog in the wheel.

I teach neither equality nor inequality – I teach uniqueness. Every individual is unique and needs to be respected in his uniqueness. Because every individual is unique, the birthright should be equal opportunity for your growth of uniqueness.

It is such a simple and obvious fact. Two thousand years have passed and you have not been able to produce another Jesus. Twenty-five centuries have passed and you have not been able to produce another Gautam Buddha. Still you go on saying man is equal?

Each individual is unique, and everybody should be respected as a world in himself. He is neither inferior to anybody nor is he superior to anybody; he is alone. In this aloneness there is beauty. You are no longer a mob, a crowd; you are yourself.

Ninth: a world government.

I am absolutely against governments. I am for one government for the whole world. That means no war will be possible; that means there will be no need to keep millions of people in armies unnecessarily. They can be productive, they can be helpful, and if they are merged into the rest of humanity all poverty will disappear.

Right now seventy percent of the national income of every country goes to the army and the rest of the country lives on thirty percent. If armies disappear, seventy percent of the income of every country will be available. There is no need to be poor, there is no need to have any beggars.

These beggars, these Ethiopias, are our creations. On the one hand we are creating big armies and on the other hand we are killing human beings through starvation. And these armies are doing nothing! They are simply professional killers, professional criminals, trained criminals. We are giving them training in how to kill. We talk about humanity, we talk about civilization, and still seventy percent of our income goes into killing.

One world government means a tremendous change, a revolution. The whole earth will be benefited by it.

Secondly, if there is one world government it becomes only functional. Right now government is not functional, it has real power. The president of a country or the prime minister of a country...in a functional government things will be different. Now you have the postmaster general; he is a functional person, he has no power. He has work, he has a function, but he has no power. There is no need. The man who heads your railways, what power does he have? The man who is the president of your airlines, what power does he have? It is functional.

If there is only one government, it will automatically become functional. Right now it cannot be, because the fear of other governments keeps you afraid: "Make your leaders strong, give all support to the leaders." But if there is no war there is no need of anybody having power – war is the cause of the need for power. And unless war disappears from the world, power cannot disappear; they are together.

A functional world government – like the post office, the railways, the airlines – will be efficient but without power. It will be a beautiful world where you don't know who the president is, who the prime minister is – they are your servants. Right now they have become your masters, and to keep their power they have to keep you always afraid. Pakistan is getting ready to fight with India, so you have to give power to the Indian leaders. China is going to attack....

Adolf Hitler has written in his autobiography that if you want to remain in power, keep people always afraid. And he is absolutely right. Sometimes mad people are also right.

And tenth: meritocracy.

Democracy has failed.

We have lived under many kinds of governments – aristocracy, monarchy, city democracies – and now we have seen the whole world getting addicted to the idea of democracy. But democracy has not solved any problems; it has increased the problems.

It was because of these problems that a man like Karl Marx supported a dictatorship of the proletariat. I am not a supporter of a dictatorship of the proletariat, but I have another idea that goes far ahead of democracy.

Democracy means government by the people, of the people, for the people – but it is only in words. In India there are more than a billion people. How can that many people have power? They have to delegate the power to somebody.

So it is not the people who rule, but the people who are chosen by them. What are your grounds for choosing? How do you manage to choose? And are you capable of choosing the right people? Have you been trained, educated for a democratic life? No, nothing has been done.

The ignorant masses can be exploited very easily by very insignificant things. For example, Nixon lost his election against Kennedy and the main reason was that Kennedy looked better on television than Nixon.

When he discovered this, Nixon improved. Before the next election he learned how to stand, how to walk, how to talk, how to dress. Even the color of your clothes will make a difference on television. If you go there in white you will look like a ghost.

People vote for arbitrary reasons…somebody speaks well, is a good orator. But that does not mean that he will make a good president. Somebody makes good shoes – do you think that will make him a good president?

It happened when Abraham Lincoln was chosen president. On the day of his inaugural address to the Senate, people were feeling very angry and hurt – because Lincoln's father was a shoemaker, and a shoemaker's son had defeated the great aristocrats. They were offended. One arrogant aristocrat could not tolerate it. Before Lincoln started speaking, he said, "Wait a minute. Do you recognize me? You used to come with your father to my house sometimes because your father made shoes for my family. You used to help him." And the whole Senate laughed. This was an effort to humiliate Lincoln.

But you cannot humiliate people like Abraham Lincoln. He said, "I am very grateful to you that you reminded me of my dead father at this moment. Because my father was the best shoemaker in the whole country, and I know that I can never be as good a president as he was a shoemaker. He is still ahead of me."

What criteria do you use? How do you manage?

That's why my idea is that the days of democracy are over. A new kind of system is needed, based on merit. We have thousands of universities all over the world. Why should ordinary, ignorant masses choose people who will be holding tremendous power for years? And now the power is so great that they can destroy the whole world.

Meritocracy means that only people who are educated in a certain area should be able to vote in that area. For example, only the educationists of the country should choose the education minister. Then you will have the best education minister possible. For the finance minister, you should choose somebody who knows finance, somebody who knows the complexities of economics. But this choice is possible only for people who are trained in economics, in financial matters – and there are thousands of people. For each post, the person who is chosen should be chosen by experts.

The health minister should be chosen by all the doctors, the surgeons, the medical experts, the scientists who are working in the medical field. Then we will have the cream of our genius, and we can depend on this cream to make the life of all humanity more peaceful, more blissful, more rich.

This is what I mean by meritocracy. And once you have chosen all the people, then those people can choose the president and the prime minister. They will be our geniuses, so they can choose the prime minister, the president. And for the parliament we should also make gradations.

For example, only people who have at least a post-graduate degree should be able to vote for the members of the parliament. Just becoming twenty-one years old does not mean you are able to choose the right person. At twenty-one years, you don't know anything about life and its complexities. At least a post-graduate degree should be held by those who choose the members of the parliament or the senate or whatever you call it. In this way, we can make an educated, refined, cultured government.

Before the world government happens, each nation should pass through a period of time when they are governed by a meritocracy. And once we have enjoyed the fruits of a meritocracy then these people will be able to understand that if we can combine the whole world into one government, life can certainly be a joy, worth living – not to renounce, but to rejoice.

Up to now, whatever has happened has been accidental. Our history up to now is nothing but a history of accidents.

We have to stop this. Now we have to decide that the future is not going to be accidental. It will be created by us; and to create our world can be the greatest creation possible.

CHAPTER 5

Proposals for Change:
A Bird's-Eye View of the Future

*I*t is the old mind, the old ideologies, the old religions -- they have all combined together to bring about the current situation of global suicide. Only a new man can save humanity and this planet, and the beautiful life of this planet.

I teach rebellion, not revolution. To me, rebelliousness is the essential quality of a religious man. It is spirituality in its absolute purity.

The future needs no more revolutions. The future needs a new experiment that has not been tried yet. Although for thousands of years there have been rebels, they remained alone, individuals. Perhaps the time was not ripe for them. But now the time is not only ripe...if you don't hurry, the time has come to an end. Either man will disappear, or a new man with a new vision will appear on the earth. He will be a rebel.

Five Dimensions of Education

The education that has prevailed in the past is very insufficient, incomplete, superficial. It only creates people who can earn their livelihood but it does not give any insight into living itself. It is not only incomplete, it is harmful too – because it is based on competition.

Any type of competition is violent deep down, and creates people who are unloving. Their whole effort is to be the achievers – of name, of fame, of all kinds of ambitions. Obviously they have to struggle and be in conflict for them. That destroys their joys and that destroys their friendliness. It seems everybody is fighting against the whole world.

Education up to now has been goal-oriented: what you are learning is not important; what is important is the examination that will come a year or two years later. It makes the future important – more important than the present. It sacrifices the present for the future. And that becomes your very style of life; you are always sacrificing the moment for something which is not present. It creates a tremendous emptiness in life.

In my vision, education will have five dimensions. Before I enter into those five dimensions, a few things have to be noted. One is that there should not be any kind of examination as part of education, but everyday, every-hour observation by the teachers. Their findings throughout the year will decide whether you move further or you remain a little longer in the same class. Nobody fails, nobody passes – it is just that a few people are speedy and a few people are a little bit lazy. The idea of failure creates a deep wound of inferiority, and the idea of being successful also creates a different kind of disease, that of superiority.

Nobody is inferior, and nobody is superior. One is just oneself, incomparable. So, examinations will not have any place. That will change the whole perspective from the future to the present. What you are doing right this moment will be decisive, not five questions at the end of two years. Of thousands of things you will pass through during these two years, each will be decisive, so the education will not be test-oriented.

The teacher has been of immense importance in the past, because he knew he had passed all the examinations, he had accumulated knowledge. But the situation has changed – and this is one of the problems, that situations change but our responses remain the old ones. Now the knowledge explosion is so vast, so tremendous, so speedy, that you cannot write a big book on any scientific subject because by the time your book is complete it will be out of date; new facts, new discoveries will have made it irrelevant. Now science has to depend on articles, on periodicals, not on books.

The teacher was educated thirty years earlier. In thirty years everything has changed, and he goes on repeating what he was taught. He is out of date, and he is making his students out of date. So in my vision the old idea of the teacher has no place. Instead of teachers there will be guides, and the difference has to be understood: the guide will tell you where, in the library, to find the latest information on the subject.

Teaching should not be done in the old-fashioned way, because television can do it in a far better way, can bring the latest information without any problems. The teacher has to appeal to your ears; television appeals directly to your eyes; and the impact is far greater, because the eyes absorb eighty percent of your life situations – they are the most alive of your senses. If you can see something there is no need to memorize it; but if you listen to something you have to memorize it.

Almost ninety-eight percent of education can be delivered through television, and the questions that students will ask can be answered by computers. The teacher should be only a guide to show you the right channel, to show you how to use the computer, how to find the latest book. His function will be totally different. He is not imparting knowledge to you, he is making you aware of the contemporary knowledge, of the latest knowledge. He is only a guide.

With these considerations, I divide education into five dimensions. The first is informative, like history, geography, and many other subjects that can be dealt with by television and computer together. The second part should be the sciences. They can be imparted by television and computer too, but they are more complicated, and the human guide will be more necessary.

In the first dimension also come languages. Every person in the world should know at least two languages; one is his mother tongue, and the other is English as an international vehicle for communication. They can also be taught more accurately by television – the accent, the grammar, everything can be taught more correctly than by individual teachers.

We can create in the world an atmosphere of brotherhood: language connects people and language disconnects too. There is right now no international language. This is due to our prejudices. English is perfectly suitable, because it is known by more people around the world on a wider scale – although it is not the language spoken by the most people. The first is Spanish, as far as population is concerned. But its population is concentrated, it is not spread all over the world. The second is Chinese, and that is even more concentrated, only in China. As far as numbers go, these languages are spoken by more people, but the question is not of numbers, the question is of spread.

English is the most widespread language, and people should drop their prejudices – they should look at the reality. There have been many efforts to create languages to avoid the prejudices – the Spanish people can say their language should be the international language because it is spoken by more people than almost any other language. To avoid these disputes, languages like Esperanto have been created. But no created language has been able to function. There are a few things that grow, which cannot be created; and language is a growth of thousands of years. Esperanto seems so artificial that all those efforts have failed.

But it is absolutely necessary to create two languages – first, the mother tongue, because there are feelings and nuances which you can say only in the mother tongue.

One of my professors, S. K. Saxena, was a world traveler who had been a professor of philosophy in many countries. He used to say that in a foreign language you can do everything, but when it comes to a fight or to love, you feel that you are not being true and sincere to your feelings. So for your feelings and for your sincerity, your mother tongue...which you imbibe with the milk of the mother, which becomes part of your blood and bones and marrow. But that is not enough – that creates small groups of people and makes others strangers.

One international language is absolutely necessary as a basis for one world, for one humanity. So two languages should be absolutely necessary for everybody. That will come in the first dimension.

The second is the enquiry into scientific subjects, which is tremendously important because science is half of reality, the outside reality.

And the third will be what is missing in present-day education, the art of living. People have taken it for granted that they know what love is. They don't know...and by the time they know, it is too late. Every child should be helped to transform his anger, hatred, jealousy, into love.

An important part of the third dimension should also be a sense of humor. Our so-called education makes people sad and serious. If one third of your life is wasted in a university in being sad and serious, it becomes ingrained; you forget the language of laughter – and the man who forgets the language of laughter has forgotten much of life.

So love, laughter, and an acquaintance with life and its wonders, its mysteries…the birds singing in the trees should not go unheard. The trees and the flowers and the stars should have a connection with your heart. The sunrise and the sunset will not be just outside things, they should be something inner, too. A reverence for life should be the foundation of the third dimension.

People are so irreverent to life. They still go on killing animals to eat – they call it "game." And if the animal eats them, then they call it a calamity! Strange…in a game, both parties should be given equal opportunity. The animals are without weapons and you have guns or arrows. You may not have thought about why arrows and guns were invented – so that you can kill the animal from a faraway distance; to come close is dangerous. What kind of game is this? And the poor animal, defenseless against your bullets....

It is not a question of killing the animals; it is a question of being irreverent to life, because all that you need can be provided either by nutritional supplements or by other scientific methods. All your needs can be fulfilled; no animal has to be killed. And a person who kills animals, deep down can kill human beings without any difficulty – because what is the difference?

A great reverence for life should be taught, because life is God and there is no other God than life itself, and joy, laughter, a sense of humor – in short a dancing spirit.

The fourth dimension should be of art and creativity: painting, music, craftsmanship, pottery, masonry, anything that is creative. All areas of creativity should be allowed; the students can choose. There should be only a few things that are compulsory – for example an international language should be compulsory; a certain capacity to earn your livelihood should be compulsory; a certain creative art should be compulsory. You can choose from the whole rainbow of creative arts, because unless a person learns how to create, he never becomes a part of existence, which is constantly creative. By being creative one becomes divine; creativity is the only prayer.

And the fifth dimension should be the art of dying. In this fifth dimension will be all the meditations, so that you can know there is no death, so that you can become aware of an eternal life inside you. This should be absolutely essential, because everybody has to die; nobody can avoid it. And under the big umbrella of meditation, you can be introduced to Zen, to Tao, to Yoga, to Hassidism, to all kinds and all possibilities that have existed, but which education has not taken any care of. In this fifth dimension, you should also be made aware of the martial arts like aikido, jujitsu, judo – the art of self-defense without weapons – and not only self-defense, but simultaneously a meditation too.

We will have a full education, a whole education. All that is essential should be compulsory, and all that is nonessential should be optional. One can choose from the options, which will be many. And once the basics are fulfilled, then you have to learn something you enjoy; music, dance, painting – you have to know something to go inwards, to know yourself. And all this can be done very easily without any difficulty.

I have been a professor myself and I resigned from the university with a note saying: This is not education, this is sheer stupidity; you are not teaching anything significant. But this insignificant education prevails all over the world. Nobody has looked for a more whole, a total education. In this sense almost everybody is uneducated; even those who have great degrees are uneducated in the vaster areas of life. A few are more uneducated, a few are less – but everybody is uneducated. But to find an educated man is impossible, because education as a whole does not exist anywhere.

Preparing People for Power

Up to now, for thousands of years you have never prepared anybody for power positions in the society. If somebody is going to be a boxer you don't just push him into the ring and say, "Start!" He has to learn. If somebody is going to be a swordsman, it will take years. Otherwise he won't even know how to hold the sword – using it and fighting with it will be impossible. First he will have to find out how to take it out from its sheath, how to hold it. It needs training. You don't just give a guitar to somebody who has never seen the instrument before and expect him to be a Yehudi Menuhin or a Ravi Shankar.

Now this is your fault: these people who are in power, have you trained them? Has anybody ever thought that the people who will be holding so much power need certain qualities so that they don't misuse power? It is not their fault.

So I propose two institutes in every university. One institute is for deprogramming. Anybody who gets a graduation certificate will first have to get a clearance from the deprogramming institute – which means that it has deprogrammed you as a Christian, as a Hindu, as a Mohammedan, as a Jew…because this has been our trouble. And four years is enough time. Deprogramming does not take that much time; just a few hours a month for four years and you will be deprogrammed. And you will not get any certificate from the educational institution unless you are first cleared by the deprogramming institute stating that "this man is now simply a human being. He is no longer a Christian, no longer a Hindu, no longer a Mohammedan, no longer a Jew."

The second institute will be an institute for meditation, because just deprogramming is not enough. Deprogramming takes rubbish from you, but you are left empty – and it is difficult to be empty; you will start gathering rubbish again. You cannot manage by yourself to learn how to live joyfully with your emptiness. That's the whole art of meditation.

So on the one hand the deprogramming institute cleanses you, empties you, makes you a vacuum; and the meditation institute goes on helping you to enjoy your nothingness, your emptiness, your inner vacuum and its cleanliness, its freshness. And as you start enjoying it you start feeling that it is not empty at all, it is full of joy. It looked empty at first because you were accustomed to having so much rubbish in it, and that rubbish has been removed so you say it looks empty.

It is just like a room full of furniture: you have always seen it full of furniture; then one day you come and all the furniture is removed and you say, "The room looks empty." The room is not empty, the room is simply clean. The room is roomy for the first time. It was cluttered before, burdened, full of rubbish; now it is pure space.

You have to learn meditation to enjoy your emptiness. And that is one of the greatest days in life – when a person starts enjoying emptiness, aloneness, nothingness.

Then nobody can reprogram you, nobody in the world. Even if Jesus comes and says to you, "You are blessed. Just come, follow me, and I will take you to God," you will say, "You go to hell with your God. Where I am, here is paradise. Wherever I am, here is paradise. You go, you follow yourself – and carry your cross also! And if nobody crucifies you, you should crucify yourself."

This is what Buddha actually said to his disciples: "If I come in the way, immediately cut off my head. I should not clutter your inner cleanliness. I should not be there, nobody should be there – no God. You alone are enough, more than enough. It is so overflowing."

So a second institute is needed in every university that will be giving you a simple meditation. There is no need for any complexity. Universities and the intelligentsia tend to make things complex. A simple method of just watching your breath is enough. But every day for one hour you have to go to the institute. Unless the meditation institute gives you its certification, the university is not going to give you a degree.

The university's degree will come only when a clearance certificate from the deprogramming institute and a graduation certificate from the meditation university have been granted. It will depend on you – you can graduate in a year, you can graduate in two years, you can graduate in three years, four years. But four years is too long. Any imbecile, if he just sits for one hour every day doing nothing for four years is bound to find what Buddha or Lao Tzu have found, what I have found. It is not a question of intelligence, talent, genius. It is only a question of patience.

So from the university meditation institute you get a degree, a bachelor of meditation; then you get a bachelor of arts or commerce or science, not before it. And in the same way it continues. You get a master's degree in meditation, and again you will be required to continue with the deprogramming institute for two years, because you can't be left so easily alone. People are, in some strange way, collectors of all kinds of things. A few people collect antiques, a few people collect stamps – postal stamps!

I was staying in a home in Madras, and the old man – he must have been sixty-five – my host, said, "Would you like to see my stamp collection?"

I said, "Your stamp collection?"

He said, "Yes, from my very childhood. But you will be surprised, I have such rare stamps."

He had a room full of all kinds of stamps. I said, "That's all you have been doing your whole life?"

He said, "You say, 'That's all?' This is the best collection in the whole country!"

I said, "It may be the best collection, but you wasted your life collecting all this rubbish, these used stamps?"

He had devoted his whole life – and he had letters of recognition from governors, from chief ministers, from prime ministers, from the president. They all had come to see his collection. Anyone of any importance who went to Madras was bound to go to see his collection; it was the best in India.

I said, "The collection is okay, but leave the collection aside; I am worried about you."

He said, "What is wrong with me? I am perfectly okay."

I said, "You are not okay! If you were an eight-year-old child it would be okay, this collection. But you are sixty-five, and you are still collecting?"

He said, "I am still collecting. I am going to collect as much as I can."

I said, "You go on collecting, but death will be coming soon: this collection will remain here and you will be gone without ever having lived because your whole time was wasted in collecting stamps."

People are collectors. I think there is some psychological necessity. Because they feel meaningless, because they feel that they are not of any worth, they try to fill this gap by collecting something. By collecting knowledge, by collecting any kind of thing, they want somehow to feel that they are not empty and they have something valuable; they are worthy, they have not wasted their life.

So if you are going to continue on to do your master's degree, then for two years you will continue with the institute of deprogramming – because there is no end to cleaning you. Every day the dust collects. It is not a question of your collecting it, it is just like a mirror: every morning you have to clean it and dust goes on collecting on it.

The mind is almost like a mirror, a reflector. Memories collect, experiences collect – this is the dust that is happening twenty-four hours a day. So unless you go on cleaning it continuously, soon you will be covered with dust again. So it is good experience: for two years again you are being deprogrammed; and for two years again you are meditating.

These processes go on simultaneously deprogramming and meditation. One goes on cleaning you, emptying you; the other goes on filling you not with some thing but some quality – blissfulness, lovingness, compassion, a tremendous feeling of worth for no reason at all. Just that you are living, breathing, is enough proof that existence thinks you worthy of living, that existence thinks you worthy of being here.

You are indispensable to existence. This indispensability is discovered only through meditation; there is no other way. And unless you discover this indispensability to existence, you are going to do something stupid to feel worthy.

But when existence overwhelms you, showers all its blessings on you, then the urge to collect garbage simply disappears. Then you live each moment and you die each moment. That is the time when meditation has come to its perfection:

Living each moment, dying each moment. Dying to the memory that you have lived, dying to the moment that is just passing. It can leave its trace, its lining, its signature, its memories – no, die to all that so you are again fresh, ready to mirror existence with a clear reflection.

So if a person continues to study in the university, then he continues to go to the meditation institute for one hour every day; and before he gets his Master's degree he gets his master of meditation certificate. He can get it in one year, he can get it in two years; or he may take a longer time if he is not meditating, because there is not going to be any verbal examination – it is going to depend on the meditation master.

If the master feels, watching you coming every day, sitting, going – for two years he watches you, inquires about you, how you are feeling, how things are going – and never sees any tension in you, never feels that you are in a hurry, anguished, worried; and that you are always relaxed, at ease, at home; that you don't feel nervous about anything; that you are not concerned about the past and not concerned about the future... Just all these things he goes on watching, and if he feels – and there is no question of misjudging. If he is a meditator, he is not going to misjudge anybody; that is impossible. He will know for sure that you have the taste of it, and he will give you the certificate.

These are clearance certificates for your master's degree. And it should continue: if you are going to do your Ph.D. then you do three years deprogramming and three years meditation. Those are compulsory to the very end, so when you come out of the university you are not only an intelligent person, well-informed, you are also a meditator – relaxed, silent, peaceful, observant, watchful, intuitive. And you are no longer a Christian, no longer a Hindu, no longer an American, no longer a Russian. All that bullshit has been completely burned, nothing is left of it.

This is the only way to replace the politicians by the intelligentsia. But as the intelligentsia is now, it won't be of much help, because they are all as much into power politics as the politicians are. That's why I make these two conditions necessary. If you get a Ph.D., simultaneously you will be getting a doctor's degree in meditation. So while you are being educated you are, in a very silent and subtle way, being prepared to be in power, in such a way that power cannot corrupt you, that you cannot misuse it.

So my vision of meritocracy is a whole program of transforming the structure of society, the structure of government, the structure of education.

It looks utopian. Who is going to do it? How is it going to happen? How are we going to make it a reality? It is utopian, but the situation is such that if things keep going as they are, politicians will bring you to the brink of death. Then you will have to choose; and at that time, when you have to choose between death and meditation, I think you will choose meditation – you are not going to choose death.

If at that time you have to choose between death and deprogramming, you will choose deprogramming: "Let the Christian die, but I can live. Let the Jew die, I can live." And who bothers when it is a question of you or the Jew? If you can choose only one, either you or the Jew, I don't think you are going to choose the Jew. Even Moses would not have done that. I trust him to have been at least that intelligent.

Politicians have brought this great challenge to the whole of humanity. In a way we should be thankful to these fools: they have dragged the whole of humanity to the point where humanity has to decide, "Now either we can live or these politicians can remain in power – both are not possible."

When you talk about power based on merit, it sounds as if you're against democracy. Are you?

It does not exist, so there is no question of my being against democracy, anti-democratic. There is no democracy, so how can I be anti-democracy? What I am proposing is the right way to change the whole structure, so that one day meritocracy can merge into democracy – because sooner or later everybody can be educated. I am not preventing anybody; I am simply saying that right now we should give the power of governing only to those who are entitled to it and prepared for it. Meanwhile, go on preparing other people.

We may not be here when it is achieved, but that does not matter. Within three or four generations, everybody can pass through a process of deprogramming, meditation and education. Then all people are entitled – because by twenty-one, most have already graduated; they can participate in the local elections. A few of them are college graduates; they can participate in the state elections. And by twenty-four, most of you are post-graduates: you can participate in all the elections. So that before you are thirty you will be able to run for the presidency of the country.

I am not asking much, just a ten-year preparation. And if the whole government is meditative, deprogrammed, unprejudiced – just visualize it – then bureaucracy disappears, hierarchy disappears; then things that take years can be finished within seconds.

Politicians and priests both have to be taken out of their long, long-standing establishment, and a totally new kind of management has to be developed. It is a difficult job, arduous but not impossible – particularly in such a situation when death is the only alternative.

A World Academy of Creative Science, Art and Consciousness

For centuries man has been told all kinds of life-negative things. Even to torture your body has been a spiritual discipline. My idea is to create an academy for science to become, for the first time, intentional and not accidental. Up to now science has been accidental. People have stumbled upon some discoveries, inventions. Even discoveries were made for which no one was looking, but as part of the scientists groping in the dark with no sense of direction. Obviously the politicians of the world – who wanted more and more destructive power in their hands – got the idea to enslave scientists.

Now every scientist is a slave to some nation, to some government and he functions only for purposes which are anti-life, destructive. The more destructive things he can find, the more he is praised by the government. An academy of creative science will consciously avoid anything that destroys life and will seek and search only for that which enhances life.

But the academy cannot be only of science, because science is only a part of human reality. The academy has to be comprehensive – it has to be for creativity, for art, for consciousness. Hence it will have three divisions, major divisions, not separated, but just for arbitrary purposes to be denominated as separate.

The most fundamental thing will be creating methods, techniques, ways of raising human consciousness – and certainly, this consciousness cannot be against the body; this consciousness is residing in the body. They cannot be seen as inimical to each other; in every way, they are supportive. I say something to you and my hand makes a gesture without my telling the hand. There is a deep synchronicity between me and my hand.

You walk, you eat, you drink and all these things indicate that you are a body and consciousness as an organic whole. You cannot torture the body and raise your consciousness. The body has to be loved – you have to be a great friend to it. It is your home, you have to clean it of all junk, and you have to remember that it is in your service continuously, day in, day out. Even when you are asleep, your body is continuously working for you digesting, changing your food into blood, taking out the dead cells from the body, bringing new oxygen, fresh oxygen into the body – and you are fast asleep!

It is doing everything for your survival, for your life, although you are so ungrateful that you have never even thanked your body. On the contrary, your religions have been teaching you to torture it: the body is your enemy and you have to get free from the body and its attachments. I also know that you are more than the body and there is no need to have any attachment. But love is not an attachment, compassion is not an attachment. Love and compassion are absolutely needed for your body and its nourishment. And the better body you have, the more is the possibility for growing consciousness. It is an organic unity.

A totally new kind of education is needed in the world where fundamentally everybody is introduced into the silences of the heart – in other words into meditations – where everybody has to be prepared to be compassionate to his or her own body. Because unless you are compassionate to your own body, you cannot be compassionate to any other body. It is a living organism, and it has done no harm to you. It has been continuously in service since you were conceived and will be till your death. It will do everything that you would like to do, even the impossible, and it will not be disobedient to you.

It is inconceivable to create such a mechanism which is so obedient and so wise. If you become aware of all the functions of your body, you will be surprised. You have never thought what your body has been doing. It is so miraculous, so mysterious. But you have never looked into it. You have never bothered to be acquainted with your own body and you pretend to love other people. You cannot, because those other people also appear to you as bodies.

The body is the greatest mystery in the whole of existence. This mystery needs to be loved – its mysteries, its functionings to be intimately inquired into.

The religions have unfortunately been absolutely against the body. But it gives a clue, a definite indication that if a man learns the wisdom of the body and the mystery of the body, he will never bother about the priest or about God. He will have found the most mysterious within himself, and within the mystery of the body is the very shrine of your consciousness.

Once you have become aware of your consciousness, of your being, there is no God above you. Only such a person can be respectful for other human beings, other living beings, because they all are as mysterious as he himself is, different expressions, varieties which make life richer. And once a man has found consciousness in himself, he has found the key to the ultimate. Any education that does not teach you to love your body, does not teach you to be compassionate to your body, does not teach you how to enter into its mysteries, will not be able to teach you how to enter into your own consciousness.

The body is the door – the body is the stepping stone. And any education that does not touch the subject of your body and consciousness is not only absolutely incomplete, it is utterly harmful because it will go on being destructive. It is only the flowering of consciousness within you that prevents you from destruction. And that gives you a tremendous urge to create – to create more beauty in the world, to create more comfort in the world. That's why I include art as the second part of the academy. Art is a conscious effort to create beauty, to discover beauty, to make your life more joyful, to teach you to dance, to celebrate.

And the third part is a creative science. Art can create beauty, science can discover objective truth, and consciousness can discover subjective reality. These three together can make any system of education complete. All else is secondary, may be useful for mundane purposes, but it is not useful for spiritual growth, it is not useful to bring you to the sources of joy, love, peace, silence. And a man who has not experienced the inner ecstasy has lived in vain unnecessarily. He vegetated, he dragged himself from the womb to the grave but he could not dance and he could not sing and he could not contribute anything to the world.

According to me a religious person is one who contributes to the world some beauty, some joy, some happiness, some celebration which was not there – something new, something fresh, some more flowers. But religion has never been defined the way I am defining it. All the ways religion has been defined have been proved absolutely ugly and wrong. But they have not helped humanity to rise to the heights of joy and beauty and love. They have drowned the whole humanity in misery and suffering, they have not taught you freedom. On the contrary, they have enforced on you all kinds of slavery in the name of obedience.

Obedience to whom? Obedience to the priests, obedience to those who have money, obedience to those who have power – in short, obedience to all the vested interests.

A small minority has been enslaving the whole humanity for centuries. Only a right education can transform this ugly and sick situation.

My idea of a World Academy of Creative Science, Art and Consciousness is really in other words my vision of a real religion. Man needs a better body, a healthier body. Man needs a more conscious, alert being. Man needs all kinds of comforts and luxuries that existence is ready to deliver. Existence is ready to give you paradise here now, but you go on postponing it – it is always after death.

In Sri Lanka one great mystic was dying...

He was worshipped by thousands of people. They gathered around him. He opened his eyes: just a few more breaths would he take on the shore and he would be gone, and gone forever.

Everybody was eager to listen to his last words. The old man said, "I have been teaching you for my whole life about blissfulness, ecstasy, meditativeness. Now I am going to the other shore. I will not be available anymore. You have listened to me, but you have never practiced what I have been telling you. You have always been postponing. But now there is no point in postponing, I am going. Is anyone ready to go with me?"

There was a great pindrop silence. People looked at each other thinking that perhaps this man who had been a disciple for forty years, thinking he may be ready. But he was looking at the others – nobody was standing up. Just from the very back a man raised his hand. The great mystic thought, "At least, one person is courageous enough."

But that man said, "Please let me make it clear to you why I am not standing up. I have only raised my hand. I want to know how to reach to the other shore, because today of course I am not ready. There are many things that are incomplete: a guest has come, my young son is getting married, and this day I cannot go – and you say from the other shore, you cannot come back.

"Some day, one day certainly, I will come and meet you. If you can just explain to us once more – although you have been explaining to us for your whole life – just once more how to reach the other shore? But please keep in mind that I am not ready to go right now. I just want to refresh my memory so that when the right time comes..."

That right time never comes.

It is not a story only about that poor man, it is the story of millions of people, of almost all. They are all waiting for the right moment, the right constellation of stars…They are consulting astrology, going to the palmist, inquiring in different ways what is going to happen tomorrow.

Tomorrow does not happen – it never has happened. It is simply a stupid strategy of postponement. What happens is always today.

A right kind of education will teach people to live here now, to create a paradise of this earth, not to wait for death to come, and not to wait for death to come, and not to be miserable till death stops your misery.

Let death find you dancing and joyous and loving. It is a strange experience that if a man can live his life as if he is already in paradise, death cannot take away anything from that man's experience.

My approach is to teach you that this is the paradise, there is no paradise anywhere else, and no preparation is needed to be happy. No discipline is needed to be loving; just a little alertness, just a little wakefulness, just a little understanding. And if education cannot give you this little understanding, it is not education.

My conception of a world academy means that the whole world should have the same education of meditation, of art, of creative science. If we can create a sane educational system around the world, then the divisions of religion and the discrimination between white and black and nations, the ugly politics that exists because of them, and the stupid behavior of men preparing continuously for war… Whenever I see a soldier I cannot believe that this man has a mind at all. Even animals don't become soldiers. But man seems to have only one interest: how to kill, how to kill more efficiently, how to go on refining instruments for killing.

A right education will teach you how to find your own song and how to learn the dance and not be shy; how to celebrate the small things of life and make this whole planet alive. It is only one, as far as we know, where people can love, where people can meditate, where people can become buddhas, where people like Socrates and Lao Tzu can exist.

We are most fortunate to be on this small planet. It is one of the smallest planets in the universe, but even the greatest stars, millions of times bigger than this earth, cannot claim a single Albert Einstein or a Jesus or a Yehudi Menuhin. It is strange that in this vast universe existence has been successful only on this small planet to create a little consciousness, a little life. Now it is in our hands to grow from this small beginning into the infinite heights which are our potential and which are our birthright.

Up to now education has not been in the right direction. It has been torturing people unnecessarily with history, with geography. If somebody is interested, these subjects should be available. If somebody is interested to know about Constantinople, then let him know. And if somebody is interested to know about Genghis Khan, Tamerlane, let him know. But there is no need to teach people compulsorily all the nonsense and garbage that has happened in the past. That is so stupid and so unbelievable.

To teach people that there have been persons like Genghis Khan and Nadirshah and Tamerlane and Alexander the Great is to teach people about the wrong side of their being.

I have been fighting in the universities, "Why don't you teach about Socrates? Why don't you teach about Chuang Tzu? Why don't you teach about Bodhidharma...?" These are the right side of consciousness. And teaching about the wrong kind of people gives you an idea that it is perfectly good if you are wrong. If you are going to be a Genghis Khan it is perfectly right. You are not doing something new, man has always been doing this.

We have to sort out history, cut out all those wrong people and protect our children from being conditioned that man has been involved in nothing but war, fighting, competition, greed. We should teach our children not what has been but what can be – not the past, but the future. Why waste so much time on teaching subjects that are of no significance in actual, existential life and not give them a single direction about the art of love, the art of life, the meaning of existence, preparation for death with joy, silence and meditativeness. All that is essential is missing, and that which is non-essential and absolutely stupid is being forced.

They say history repeats. History does not repeat; it is our stupidity that we go on and on teaching the same thing to each generation. The poor children are conditioned to imitate the same great heroes who were really criminals, not heroes. Just a single man, Genghis Khan, killed forty million people. It is better to drop all information about these people from education. Give an education about the dance of a Shiva, the flute of Krishna. Teach them all that has been beautiful and good so that they become accustomed that all that is good is natural, and the bad is accidental – that the bad does not happen, has never happened, and the good is absolutely normal. To be a buddha is not something abnormal. It should be taught to every child that to be a buddha is a normal phenomenon. Anybody who is wise enough is going to become a buddha.

You are going to become a buddha. The greatest revolution has to happen in education and its systems; otherwise, man will go on repeating history.

Now time for silence and time for laughter....

Hymie Goldberg comes home from work one evening and Becky says, "Did you go to the store and pick up the snapshots, like I asked you? You probably did not! You never listen to me! You never remember anything! Oh! You did get them. Well, thank goodness for miracles. Let me see them! This shot is terrible and this one is even worse. My God! This one is horrible and this one is a disaster. In fact, this is the worst lot of photographs I have ever seen in my life.

"You can't do anything right! You can't drive a car properly! You can't even change a fuse. You can't sing in tune, and as a photographer, you are the worst!

"Just take a look at these pictures: in every one you took of me, I have my mouth open!"

A reformed prostitute is giving testimony on a street corner with the Salvation Army. She punctuates her talk by beating on a big drum.

"I used to be a sinner!" she shouts.

BOOM! goes the drum.

"I used to be a bad woman!" she cries.

BOOM!

"I used to drink!"

BOOM!

"Gamble!"

BOOM!

"Chase men!"

BOOM! BOOM!

"I used to go wild on Saturday nights and raise hell!"

BOOM! BOOM! BOOM!

"And now what do I do on Saturday nights?" she cries. "I stand on the street corner beating this fucking drum!"

No Religions but a Quality of Religiousness

I teach not religion, but religiousness – a flowing river, continuously changing its course, but ultimately reaching the ocean.

Religion is a dead rock. A rock may be very ancient, far more experienced, far older than any Rigveda, but a rock is a rock, and it is dead. It does not move with the seasons, it does not move with existence; it is simply lying there. And have you seen any rock with any song, with any dance?

To me religion is a quality, not an organization.

All the religions that exist in the world – and they are not a small number, there are three hundred religions in the world – are dead rocks. They don't flow, they don't change, they don't move with the times. And anything that is dead is not going to help you – unless you want to make a grave, and then perhaps the rock may be helpful. All the so-called religions have been making graves for you, destroying your life, your love, your joy, and filling your heads with fantasies, illusions, hallucinations about God, about heaven and hell, about reincarnation, and all kinds of crap.

I trust the flowing, changing, moving...because that is the nature of life. It knows only one thing permanent, and that is change. Only change never changes; otherwise, everything changes. Sometimes it is fall and the trees become naked. All the leaves fall down with no complaint; silently, peacefully, they merge back into the earth from where they have come. The naked trees against the sky have a beauty of their own, and a tremendous trust must be there in their hearts because they know that if the old leaves are gone, the new will be coming. And soon new leaves, fresh, younger, more delicate, start coming out.

A religion should not be a dead organization but a kind of religiousness, a quality – which includes truthfulness, sincerity, naturalness, a deep let-go with the cosmos, a loving heart, a friendliness towards the whole. For these, no holy scriptures are needed.

In fact, there are no holy scriptures anywhere. The so-called holy scriptures do not even prove that they are good literature! It is good that nobody reads them, because they are full of ugly pornography. One of my friends, when I said this, started researching the Holy Bible, and he has found five hundred solid pages of pornography. If any book has to be banned from the world, it is the Holy Bible! But that friend does not know that the Bible is just nothing. If you look into the Hindu *Puranas*, you will be surprised; they are the most ancient editions of Playboy Magazine! Not only the human beings but even the gods described there are such ugly, dirty old men, it is strange…and they are still worshipped as gods.

For example, the moon is worshipped as a god by the Hindus and by the Jainas, but the story is that the moon was sexually interested in a beautiful woman, who was the wife of a saint. In India the saints go to take a bath early in the morning before the sun rises, and that was the time when the moon would come – of course in disguise, because gods can do anything. He would knock on the door and the wife would think her husband was back. The moon would make love to somebody else's wife and then disappear.

Almost all the so-called Hindu gods are rapists. And they are not satisfied that in heaven they have the most beautiful women – not covered with skin, but covered with plastic. But they had no word for plastic in those days, it seems. They say that the heavenly girls – the word is *apsara*, which you can translate very accurately as a "call girl"; they are not ordinary prostitutes, but very high class – don't perspire. When I came to know this – that they don't perspire – I started wondering, how is it possible for a man or woman with skin not to perspire? Plastic seems to be the only explanation. And they also remain stuck at the age of sixteen; they never grow up. For centuries they have been only sixteen… And how many saints have enjoyed them? I don't think they can even calculate the number over millions of years.

An authentic religiousness needs no prophets, no saviors, no holy books, no churches, no popes, no priests – because religiousness is the flowering of your heart. It is reaching to the very center of your being. And the moment you reach to the very center of your being, there is an explosion of beauty, of blissfulness, of silence, of light. You start becoming a totally different person. All that was dark in your life disappears, and all that was wrong in your life disappears too. Whatever you do is done with utter totality and absolute awareness.

I know only of one virtue, and that is awareness.

If religiousness spreads all over the world, religions will fade away. And it will be a tremendous blessing to humanity when man is simply man, neither Christian nor Mohammedan nor Hindu. These demarcations, these divisions have been the cause of thousands of wars all through history. If you look back at the history of man, you cannot resist the temptation to say that we have lived in the past in an insane way. In the name of God, in the name of church, in the name of ideologies that have no support in reality at all, people have been killing each other.

Religion has not happened to the world yet. Unless religiousness becomes the very climate of humanity there will be no religion at all. But I insist on calling it religiousness so that it does not become organized.

You cannot organize love. Have you ever heard of churches of love, temples of love, mosques of love? Love is an individual affair with another individual. And religiousness is a greater love affair between the individual and the whole cosmos. When a person falls in love with the whole cosmos – the trees, the mountains, the rivers, the oceans, the stars – that person knows what prayer is. It is wordless. He knows a deep dance in his heart, and a music that has no sound. He experiences for the first time the eternal, the immortal, that which always remains through every change – that which renews its life afresh. And anyone who becomes a religious person and drops Christianity, Hinduism, Mohammedanism, Jainism, Buddhism, for the first time declares his individuality.

Religiousness is an individual affair. It is a message of love from you to the whole cosmos. Only then will there be a peace that passeth all misunderstanding. Otherwise these religions have been parasites exploiting people, enslaving people, forcing people to believe. And all beliefs are against intelligence, forcing people to pray words that have no meaning because they are not coming from your heart, but only from your memory.

I have often told the beautiful story of Leo Tolstoy. The story is about three villagers, uneducated, uncultured, who lived on a small island in a big lake. Thousands of people were going to them, worshipping them, and the archbishop became concerned. The churches were empty, nobody was coming to hear the archbishop. And the Russian church is the oldest in the world, very orthodox, and people were going to those three persons who were not even initiated into the secrets of Christianity – how had they become saints?

In India it is easy to become a saint, but in Christianity it is not so easy. The English word "saint" comes from a root, sanctus. It means that unless you are sanctioned, certified by the pope, you cannot be accepted as a saint. But people were saying those three people were so saintly....

In anger one day the archbishop took a boat and went to see those three people, who were sitting under a tree. He looked at them and he could not believe it: what kind of saints are these? He introduced himself and declared, "I am the archbishop." The three saints all touched his feet. Now he felt relaxed, "These are fools...and things are not yet gone so far that they cannot be controlled."

He asked them, "Are you saints?"

They looked at each other, and they said, "We have never heard the word. We are uneducated, uncultured. Don't talk Greek to us; just simply say what you mean."

"My God," said the archbishop, "you don't know what a saint means? Do you know the Christian prayer?"

Again they looked at each other, and nudged each other as if to say, "You tell him."

The archbishop now felt really powerful. He said, "Tell me what your prayer is."

They said, "We are very uneducated, we don't know what Christian prayer is. We have made up a prayer of our own."

The archbishop laughed. He said, "Nobody makes up his own prayer. Prayer has to be authorized by the church. What is your prayer, anyway?"

They felt very embarrassed, very shy, and finally one said, "Because you are asking, we cannot refuse. But our prayer is not much of a prayer... We have heard that God has three forms – God, the Holy Ghost, and the Son – so we thought to make a prayer of our own. Our prayer is: You are three, we are three, have mercy on us."

The archbishop said, "You idiots, do you think this is a prayer? I will teach you the prayer authorized by the church."

But the prayer was so long, and all the three spoke together: "This such a long prayer that we cannot remember it. We will try our best, but please repeat it one time more." Then they asked him to repeat it a third time, because it was so big. "If we remember the beginning, we forget the end. If we remember the end, we forget the beginning. If we remember the beginning and the end, we forget the middle."

The archbishop said, "You need education."

But they said, "We cannot write, otherwise we could have written down your prayer and read it. Just one time more... we will try our best."

The archbishop was very happy that he had converted these three idiots who were being worshipped by thousands of people. He repeated the prayer a third time, they touched his feet, and he went back into his boat.

Just as he was in the middle of the lake he saw a huge something coming towards him. He could not figure it out, "What could it be?" He started praying. As it came close, he understood that it was those three idiots ... walking on the water! He said, "My God, only Jesus has ever walked on water."

They came with folded hands saying, "We forgot the prayer, so we thought...can you repeat it one more time?"

The archbishop, seeing them standing on the water, realized the truth. He said, "You don't need my prayer. Your prayer is perfect. I have been praying my whole life, I have reached the highest post in the Orthodox Church of Russia, but I cannot walk on water. God seems to be with you. You just go and do your old prayer."

They were very happy. They said, "We are so grateful, because that long prayer would have killed us!"

It is a beautiful story, showing how it is that the traditional, the orthodox religion becomes dead. Religiousness has to arise within your heart as an individual offering of love and fragrance to the cosmos.

Even God is not necessary for a religious person, because God is an unproved hypothesis, and a religious person cannot accept anything unproved. He can accept only that which he feels. What do you feel? – the breathing, the heartbeat. The existence breathes in and out, the existence goes on giving you your life every moment. But you have never looked at the trees, you have never looked at the flowers and their beauty, and you have never thought that they are divine. They are really the only God that exists.

This whole existence is full of godliness.

If you are full of religiousness, the whole existence simultaneously becomes full of godliness.

To me, this is what religion is.

You often say we need to take care of ourselves before we try to take care of others. This seems to go against many of the religions in the world that teach service to humanity and it must appear a very selfish attitude to them. Can you speak on this?

It not only goes against many religions, it goes against all the religions in the world. They all teach service to others, unselfishness. But to me, selfishness is a natural phenomenon. Unselfishness is imposed. Selfishness is part of your nature. Unless you come to a point where your self dissolves into the universal, you cannot be truly unselfish. You can pretend. You will be only a hypocrite, and I don't want people to be hypocrites. So it is a little complicated, but it can be understood.

First, selfishness is part of your nature. You have to accept it. And if it is part of your nature it must be serving something essential, otherwise it would not have been there at all. It is because of selfishness that you have survived, that you have taken care of yourself; otherwise humanity would have disappeared long ago.

Just think of a child who is unselfish, born unselfish. He will not be able to survive, he will die – because even to breathe is selfish, to eat is selfish, when there are millions of people who are hungry and you are eating, when there are millions of people who are unhealthy, sick, dying, and you are healthy.

If a child is born without selfishness as an intrinsic part of his nature, he is not going to survive. If a snake comes close to him, what is the need to avoid the snake? Let him bite. It is your selfishness that protects you; otherwise, you are coming in the way of the snake. If a lion jumps upon you and kills you, be killed. That is unselfishness. The lion is hungry, you are providing food – who are you to interfere? You should not protect yourself, you should not fight. You should simply offer yourself on a plate to the lion. That will be unselfishness. All these religions have been teaching things that are unnatural. This is only one of the things.

I teach nature. I teach you to be natural, absolutely natural, unashamedly natural. Yes, I teach you selfishness. Nobody has said it before, they had not the guts to say it. And they were all selfish; this is the amazing part of the whole story.

Why is a Jaina monk torturing himself? There is a motivation. He wants to attain to ultimate freedom, moksha, and to all the pleasures therein. He is not sacrificing anything, he is simply bargaining. He is a businessman; his scriptures say, "You will get a thousandfold." And this life is really very small – seventy years is not much. If you sacrifice seventy years of pleasures for an eternity of pleasures it is a good bargain. I don't think it is unselfish.

And why have these religions been teaching you to serve humanity? What is the motive? What is the goal? What are you going to gain out of it? You may never have asked the question. It is not service....

I have loved a very ancient Chinese story: A man falls into a well. It was at a big gathering, a big festival time, and there was so much noise, and people were enjoying, dancing, singing, and all kinds of things were going on, so nobody heard him fall. And at that time in China wells were not protected by a wall surrounding them, at least four or five feet high so nobody falls in. They were without any protection, just open. You can fall in the darkness without being aware that there is a well. The man starts shouting, "Save me!"

A Buddhist monk passes by. Of course a Buddhist monk is not interested in the festival, is not supposed to be interested – l don't know what he was doing there. Even to be there means some unconscious urge to see what is going on, how people are enjoying: "All these people will go to hell, and I am the only one here who is going to heaven."

He passes by the well and he hears this man. He looks down. The man says, "It's good that you have heard me. Everybody is so busy and there is so much noise that I was afraid I was going to die."

The Buddhist monk said, "You are still going to die, because this is your past life's evil act: now you are getting the punishment. Get it and be finished! It is good. In the new life you will come out clean and there will be no need fall again into a well."

The man said, "I don't want any wisdom and any philosophy at this moment...." But the monk had moved on.

A Taoist old man stops. He is thirsty, and looks in the well. The man is still crying for help. The Taoist says, "This is not manly. One should accept everything as it comes – that's what the great Lao Tzu has said. So accept it! Enjoy! You are crying like a woman. Be a man!"

The man said, "I am ready to be called a woman but first please save me! I am not manly. And you can say anything that you want to say afterwards – first pull me out."

But the Taoist said, "We never interfere in anybody's business. We believe in the individual and his freedom. It is your freedom to fall in the well, it is your freedom to die in the well. All that I can do is just suggest to you: you can die crying, weeping – that is foolish – or you can die like a wise man. Accept it, enjoy it, sing a song, and go. Anyway, everybody is going to die, so what is the point of saving you? I am going to die, everybody is going to die – perhaps tomorrow, perhaps the day after tomorrow – so what is the point of bothering to save you?" And he moves on.

A Confucian comes and the man sees some hope because Confucians are more worldly, more earthbound. He says, "It is my good fortune that you have come, a Confucian scholar. I know you, I have heard about your name. Now do something for me, because Confucius says, 'Help others.'" Seeing the response of the Buddhist and the Taoist, the man thought, "It is better to talk philosophy if these people are to be convinced to save me." He said, "Confucius says, 'Help others.'"

The Confucian monk said, "You are right. And I will help. I am going from one city to another, and I will try and protest and force the government to make a protective wall around every well in the country. Don't be afraid."

The man said, "But by the time those protective walls are made and your revolution succeeds, I will be gone."

The Confucian said, "You don't matter, I don't matter, individuals don't matter – society matters. You have raised a very significant question by falling in the well. Now we are going to fight for it. You be calm and quiet. We will see that every well has a protective wall around it so nobody falls into it. Just by saving you, what is saved? The whole country has millions of wells, and millions of people can fall into them. So don't be too selfish about yourself, rise above the selfish attitude. I am going to serve humanity. You have served by falling into the well. I am going to serve by forcing the government to make protective walls." And he walks on. But he makes a significant point: "You are very selfish. You just want to be saved and waste my time, which I can use for the whole of humanity."

Do you know if anything like "humanity" exists anywhere, if anything like a "society" exists anywhere? These are just words. Only individuals exist.

The fourth man is a Christian minister, a missionary, who is carrying a bag with him. He immediately opens the bag, takes out a rope, throws the rope; before the man says anything, he throws the rope into the well. The man is surprised. He says, "Your religion seems to be the truest religion."

He says, "Of course. We are prepared for every emergency. Knowing that people can fall into wells, I am carrying this rope to save them because only by saving them can I save myself. But remember – I have heard what the Confucian was saying – don't make protective walls around the wells; otherwise how will we serve humanity? How will we pull out people of wells when they fall in? They have to fall first, only then can we pull them out. We exist to serve, but the opportunity must be there. Without the opportunity, how can you serve?"

All these religions talking about service are certainly interested that humanity remains poor, that people remain in need of service, that there are orphans, there are widows, old people nobody takes care of, beggars. These people are needed, absolutely needed. Otherwise, what will happen to these great servants of the people? What will happen to all these religions and their teachings? And how will people enter into the kingdom of God? These people have to be used as a ladder.

Do you call it unselfishness? Is this missionary unselfish? He is saving this man, not for this man's sake; he is saving this man for his own sake. Deep down it is still selfishness, but now it is covered with a beautiful word: unselfishness, service.

But why is there any need for service? Why should there be any need? Can't we destroy these opportunities for service? We can, but the religions will be very angry. Their whole ground will be lost – this is their whole business – if there is nobody poor, nobody hungry, nobody suffering, nobody sick. And science can make it possible. It is absolutely in our hands today. It would have been long ago, if these religions had not stopped every person who was going to contribute to knowledge, which can destroy all the opportunities for service. But these religions have been against all scientific progress and they will talk of service. They need these people. Their need is not unselfish; it is utterly selfish. It is motivated. There is a goal to be achieved.

Hence I say to my people, service is a dirty, four letter word. Never use it. Yes, you can share, but never humiliate anybody by serving him. It is humiliation.

When you serve somebody and you feel great, you have reduced the other into a worm, subhuman. And you are so superior that you have sacrificed your own interests and you are serving the poor: you are simply humiliating them.

If you have something, something that gives you joy, peace, ecstasy, share it. And remember that when you share there is no motive. I am not saying that by sharing it you will reach to heaven. I am not giving you any goal. I am saying to you, just by sharing it you will be tremendously fulfilled. In the very sharing is the fulfillment, there is no goal beyond it. It is not end-oriented, it is an end unto itself.

And you will feel obliged to the person who was ready to share with you. You will not feel that he is obliged to you – because you have not served. And only these people who believe in sharing instead of service can destroy all those ugly opportunities which surround the whole earth. The religions have been exploiting those opportunities, but they give good names to them. They have become very proficient, over thousands of years, in giving good names to ugly things. And when you start giving a beautiful name to an ugly thing, there is a possibility you yourself may forget that it was just a cover and the ugly reality remains just the same.

Why serve the poor when poverty can be destroyed? No religion says, "Destroy poverty." They are in deep conspiracy with the vested interests. They don't say destroy poverty. They don't suggest any measures for how poverty can be solved. But they tell you to serve the poor, serve the widows.

In India, they don't ask why their culture forces the woman to remain a widow. So simple a phenomenon... In India the man is allowed to get married as many times as he wants. In fact the moment the wife dies, her body is being burned on the funeral pyre and people are beginning to talk about the man's next marriage, how to arrange a new wife for this man. So ugly, so inhuman – the body of the wife is not yet burned completely, but sitting around the funeral pyre, what else to do? They have to talk about something, and this is the hottest topic. Now this man needs a woman, and they are suggesting where it will be good to marry, which woman will be suitable for him – and it must not be a widow.

Nobody is ready to get married to a widow. She is a used woman, a thing, used by somebody else – how can you marry her? The man is not used; he always remains fresh, pure. He can get remarried. In India for thousands of years the woman has suffered so much because of this idea that she has to remain a widow. Millions of widows...they cannot wear any other color than white. They have to shave their heads, they cannot wear any ornaments. In every possible way it has been made clear to them that they have to live almost a dead life.

They cannot move in the society as other women do – particularly in festivals they are not supposed to. At marriages they are not supposed to be present, because their very presence, their very shadow, is a calamity. And the widow is told that she has eaten her husband – it is because of her fate that the husband died. If he had not married her he would be alive; she is responsible for his death. The rest of her life she carries this burden, and now she has to remain in every way ugly.

"Serve the widows." In India there are institutions especially for widows, because in homes they are not even equal to the servants. They do all kinds of work, the whole day long they work but they don't get any respect: no salary, no respect, and continual condemnation that because of them somebody's son has died, somebody's brother has died. And she has to remain hidden like a shadow. She is not allowed to be there when guests come to the house. She lives like a ghost.

So institutions are opened by religions; this is "service for the widows." But why have widows in the first place? It is such a simple logic: make it a law that any man who wants to marry a second time has to marry a widow, not a virgin – simple! And the whole problem disappears. Rather than making the problems disappear, you help them to continue.

Don't Serve the Poor, Solve the Problems

Solve the problems! There is no need of teaching people service. What are the problems? The population explosion is a problem. All the religions are teaching, "Serve the poor," but nobody is ready to say, "Accept birth control so that the population is reduced."

I am for absolute birth control. Only a few people should be allowed to give birth to children, and that too should be done by artificial insemination. ...Because what is the need? It is possible you fall in love with a girl, the girl falls in love with you, but you may not be the right persons to become parents, to give birth to a child. You may not be, because love takes no account of your inner chemistry.

You don't go to the chemist to find out, "I am falling in love with this girl; do our inner chemistries meet?" If you go at all, you go to the astrologer, the palmist...the blind leading the blind. It is a biochemical question, nothing to do with palmistry, nothing to do with astrology. But man's ego feels as if stars are interested in you. Just think of the stupidity of the whole idea that millions of stars are concerned with you, and are affecting you, and their combinations are affecting you. It just makes me feel sad about man. What kind of humanity has grown up on the earth?

But all these religions are against birth control, and without birth control there is no way now. I am in support of absolute birth control, remember, not just birth control; because with birth control people – if not religions, then governments – at best could be compelled to accept that they should have only two children or three children. No, that won't do. Even two, three children won't do. Absolute birth control: nobody is to be allowed to give birth to children; anybody who is interested in children can go, contribute his semen to the scientific lab, and the lab should decide who is going to be the woman for your child's mother.

It need not be your wife, there is no relevance in it. You love your wife, your wife loves you, but that does not mean you should burden the earth with a crippled, blind child. You don't have that power, you don't have that permission from existence. Why are you taking such an irresponsible burden on yourself and on the whole of humanity? You give birth to a child who is crippled, or blind, or mad, or insane, and he will give birth to other children.

That's how idiots are always in the majority in the world. They are bound to be, because the right combination can happen only through a scientific lab. You don't know what you are carrying in your genes; you don't know what your potential is, what kind of child you are going to give birth to. You love the woman – there is no harm in that; love should be absolutely available to you, that is your birthright. You love the woman; but every woman need not be a mother, every man need not be a father. Soon there will be no need for the mother either. The child can grow in the scientific lab itself.

You want a child, and if you really love children, you would like the best child possible. So who contributes the semen and who contributes the mother's womb should not be your concern. Your concern should be that you get the best child possible. So I suggest artificial insemination and test-tube babies. And I also suggest euthanasia.

Just as we are putting a barrier on birth, birth control, let me give you another word: death-control. After a certain age – for example, if you accept seventy as the average, or eighty or ninety as the average – a man should be free to ask the medical board, "I want to be freed from my body." He has every right, if he does not want to live anymore, because he has lived enough; he has done everything that he wanted to do. And now he wants not to die of cancer, or tuberculosis; he simply wants a relaxed death.

Every hospital should have a special place for people, with a special staff, where people can come, get relaxed and be helped to die beautifully, without any disease, supported by the medical profession. If the medical board feels that the person is valuable – for example, somebody like Einstein or Bertrand Russell – if the medical board feels that the person is of immense importance, then he can be asked to live a little longer. Only a few people should be asked to be here a little longer because they can be so much help to humanity, so much help to others. But if even those people don't want to live, that is their birthright. You can pray, ask, request. If they accept it, good. But if they say, "No, we are not interested any more," then certainly they have every right to die.

Why should a person be forced to live when he does not want to live? And you make it a crime, you make the man unnecessarily worried: he does not want to live but he has to live because suicide is a crime. He has to take poison, or he has to jump into the ocean or from a hill. This is not a good situation. And strange: if he dies, good; if he is caught then he will be sentenced to death. Great society! Great minds creating laws! He will be sentenced to death because he was trying to commit suicide.

All these problems can be solved. Hence there is no need for public servants, missionaries, and their kind. We need more intelligence brought to the problem and how to dissolve it.

So I teach selfishness. I want you to be, first, your own flowering. Yes, it will appear as selfishness; I have no objection to that appearance of selfishness. It is okay with me. But is the rose selfish when it blossoms? Is the lotus selfish when it blossoms? Is the sun selfish when it shines? So why should you be worried about selfishness?

You are born: birth is only an opportunity, just a beginning, not the end. You have to flower. Don't waste it in any kind of stupid service. Your first and foremost responsibility is to blossom, to become fully conscious, aware, alert; and in that consciousness you will be able to see what you can share, how you can solve problems.

Ninety-nine percent of the world's problems can be solved. Perhaps one percent of problems may not be solved. Then you can share with those people whatsoever you can share – but first you have to have something to share.

All these religions up to now have not helped humanity in solving a single problem. Just look at what I am saying: have they solved a single problem? – and they have been doing this service business for millions of years. The poor are still poor, and go on growing more poor. The sick are there, old age is there, all kinds of diseases are there, all kinds of crimes are there – and they go on increasing. Every year there are more crimes in the world than the last year. Strange…prisons go on increasing, courts go on increasing – they think they are there to stop crime, and with them the crime goes on increasing.

Something is basically wrong somewhere. What they are doing is unrelated to the problem. The person who is committing a crime is not a criminal, he is a sick person. He need not be thrown into a jail and tortured, he has to be put into a psychiatric hospital and served there, medically, respectfully. It is not his fault.

You must know there was a time when mad people were thought to be criminals and they were thrown into prison, and there they were beaten. It was only a few hundred years ago that it occurred to anyone that these people are not criminals, they are suffering from a certain disease. By beating them you cannot beat the disease out. You are simply being idiotic. They need treatment, and you are mistreating them. And the same is true about all criminals…because I don't see that any criminal is a born criminal. The way he is brought up, the society in which he is brought up, makes him a criminal. And once his mind starts becoming criminal, then you have to change the whole way of his mind. It is no use chaining him, throwing him into jail, starving him, beating him – it does nothing. It is simply reinforcing in him that when he comes out he will be a confirmed criminal, a graduate criminal.

Your imprisonments, your prisons, are universities for criminals, from which they graduate. So once a man goes to the jail, he comes out having learned many things from old criminals with whom he has been there. And all that he learns from your behavior is that to commit the crime is not the crime, but to be caught is the crime. So he learns ways not to be caught.

You have to change the track of his mind which moves into criminality. And that can be done. Biochemistry can be of much help, medicine can be of much help, psychiatry can be of much help. Now we have every resource to make that man a dignified human being.

Service is not needed, what is needed is a sharing of your consciousness – your knowledge, your being, your respect – but first you must have it.

To me the greatest problem with humanity is that they don't know anything of meditation. To me, that is the greatest problem. Neither the population, nor the atom bomb, nor hunger...no, these are not basic problems; they can be easily solved by science.

The only, basic problem that science will not be able to solve is that people don't know how to meditate.

To my people I say: first you be selfish, utterly selfish – blossom. Come to flowering and fragrance, and then spread it. Then share it with those unfortunate people who had the same potential as you, but life has not given them a chance to go inwards, to have a taste of their own godliness.

I am against all the religions because to me, what they have done is absolutely useless. You can use beautiful words, beautiful phrases to hide some ugly truth. I don't want to do that kind of job at all.

I teach you to be natural, and I teach you to accept your naturalness.

I know one thing for certain, that when you have blossomed, you will be sharing. There is no way to avoid it. When the flower opens up there is no way for it to withhold its fragrance and keep it imprisoned. The fragrance escapes. It reaches in all directions. So first, be fulfilled, be content. First, be. Then out of your being there will be a fragrance reaching to many. And it will not be a service, it will be a sheer joyous sharing. And there is nothing more joyful than sharing your joy.

Crime and Punishment

All legal systems are nothing but the revenge of society – revenge against those who don't fit in with the system. According to me, law is not for protection of the just, it is for protection of the crowd mind; whether it is just or unjust does not matter. Law is against the individual and for the crowd. It is an effort to reduce the individual and his freedom, and his possibility of being himself.

The latest scientific research is very revealing. Many of the people who are termed criminals are not responsible for their crimes; their crimes are genetic, they inherit them. Just as a blind man is not responsible for his blindness, a murderer is not responsible for his murderousness. Both inherit the tendency – one of blindness, another of committing murder. Now it is almost an established scientific fact that punishing anybody for any crime is simply idiotic. It is almost like punishing somebody because he has tuberculosis, or sending him to jail because he is suffering from cancer.

All criminals are sick, psychologically and spiritually both.

In my vision, the courts will not consist of law experts, they will consist of people who understand genetics and how crimes are inherited from generation to generation. They have to decide not for any punishment, because every punishment is wrong – not only wrong, every punishment is criminal. The person who has committed something wrong has to be sent to the right institution – maybe a hospital to be treated, or a psychiatric institution, or a therapeutic school. The person needs our sympathy, our love, our help. Instead of giving him our sympathy and love, for centuries we have been giving him punishment. Man has committed so much cruelty behind such beautiful names as order, law, justice.

The new man will not have any jails and will not have any judges and will not have any legal experts. These are absolutely unnecessary, cancerous growths on the body of society. There will certainly have to be sympathetic scientists, meditative, compassionate beings, to work out why it happened that a certain man committed rape. Is he really responsible? According to me, on no account is he responsible. Either he has committed rape because of the priests and the religions teaching celibacy, repression for thousands of years – this is the outcome of a repressive morality – or biologically he has hormones which compel him to commit rape.

Although you are living in a modern society, most of you are not contemporaries because you are not aware of the reality that science goes on discovering. Your educational system prevents you from knowing it, your religions prevent you from knowing it, your governments prevent you from knowing it.

A man is attracted to a woman and thinks that he is in love. The woman also thinks she is in love. But the scientific truth is that they both have certain biological factors, certain hormones that attract each other. That's why it is possible to change the sex of one person from man to woman or from woman to man just by changing the hormonal system. A good injection of hormones and you are full of love.

The man who is committing rape perhaps has more hormones than those moral people who manage to live with one woman for their whole life, thinking that they are moral. The real fact is that their hormones are weak; it is enough for their hormones to be satisfied with one woman. A man with more hormones will need more women; the same will be the case with a woman. It is not a question of morality, it is a question of biology. A man who commits rape needs our sympathy, needs a certain treatment in which his extra hormones are removed, and he will cool down, calm down – he will become a Gautam Buddha. To punish him is simply an exercise in stupidity. By punishing, you cannot change his hormones. Throwing him in jail, you will create a homosexual, or some kind of pervert. In American jails they have done a survey: thirty percent of the inmates are homosexuals. That is according to their confession; we don't know how many have not confessed. Thirty percent is not a small number. In monasteries the number is bigger – fifty percent, sixty percent. But the responsibility lies with our idiotic clinging to religions which are out of date, which are not supported and nourished by scientific research.

The new community of man will be based on science, not on superstition. If somebody does something which is harmful to the community as such, then his body has to be looked into; he needs some physiological change or biological change. His mind has to be looked into – perhaps he needs some psychoanalysis. The deepest possibility is that neither the body nor the mind are of much help; that means he needs a deep spiritual regeneration, a deep meditative cleansing.

Instead of courts, we should have meditative centers of different kinds, so every unique individual can find his own way. Instead of law experts – who are simply irrelevant, they are parasites sucking our blood – we need scientific people of different persuasions in the courts. Because somebody may have a chemical defect, somebody may have a biological defect, somebody may have a psychological defect. We need all these kinds of experts, of all persuasions and schools of psychology, all types of meditators, and we can transform the poor people who have been victims of unknown forces and have always been punished by us. They have suffered in a double sense.

First, they are suffering from an unknown biological force. Secondly, they are suffering at the hands of your judges, who are nothing but butchers, henchmen; your advocates, all kinds of your law experts, your jailers – it is simply so insane that future human beings will not be able to believe it. It is almost the same with the past.

Just the other day there was a report from South India that a woman was thought to be having intercourse with the devil. Now the devil has been almost dead for many centuries; suddenly he became alive in that small village. And the villagers took the woman to the priest who declared that she should be hung upside down from a tree and beaten because the devil was still inside her. Somebody informed the police of the nearby town. The police arrived, but the villagers were reluctant. Two hundred villagers were standing in the way, stopping the police, saying, "You cannot interfere with our religious ceremonies." They were beating the woman – and they killed her! Until she was dead, they were not satisfied. They could not find the devil, but they killed the woman.

This used to be the common practice all over the world. Mad people were beaten to cure their madness. People who were schizophrenic, who were thought to be possessed by ghosts, were beaten almost to death – this was thought to be treatment. Millions of people have died because of your great treatments.

Now we can simply say that those people were barbarous, ignorant, primitive. The same will be said about us. I am already saying it – that your courts are barbarous, your laws are barbarous. The very idea of punishment is unscientific. There is nobody in the world who is a criminal; everybody is sick, and needs sympathy and a scientific cure. Then the other half of your crimes will disappear. The first half will disappear with the disappearance of private property, because private property creates thieves, pickpockets, politicians, priests. All your politicians are pickpockets, are hoodlums. They also need psychiatric treatment, they also need to be placed in sympathetic psychiatric nursing homes. They have to be cured of their politics. Politics is a disease.

Man has suffered from many diseases and he has not even been aware that they are diseases. He has been punishing small criminals and he has been worshiping great criminals. Who is Alexander the Great? – a great criminal; he murdered people on a mass scale. Napoleon Bonaparte, Ivan the Terrible, Nadir Shah, Genghis Khan, Tamerlane are all mass scale criminals. But their crimes are so big, perhaps, that you cannot conceive… They have killed millions of people, burned millions of people alive, but they are not thought of as criminals.

And a small pickpocket, who takes away a dollar from your pocket will be punished by the court. And perhaps the dollar that you were carrying was not even authentic! But his mother is dying, and he has no money for medicine, and I cannot say that he is a criminal; he is simply a kind-hearted man who loves his mother.

Once private property disappears and everything belongs to all, naturally stealing will disappear. You don't steal water and accumulate it, you don't steal air. We have to create everything in such abundance that even a stupid person cannot think of accumulating it. What is the point? It is always available, fresh. Money has to disappear from society. A commune does not need money. Your needs should be fulfilled by the commune. All have to produce, and all have to make the commune richer, affluent, accepting the fact that a few people will be lazy. But there is no harm in it.

In every family, you will find somebody lazy. Somebody is a poet, somebody is a painter, somebody simply goes on playing on his flute – but you love the person. A certain percentage of lazy people will be respectfully allowed. In fact a commune that does not have lazy people will be a little less rich than other communes that have a few lazy people who do nothing but meditate, who do nothing but go on playing on their guitar while others are toiling in the fields. A little more human outlook is needed; these people are not useless. They may not seem to be productive of commodities, but they are producing a certain joyful, cheerful atmosphere. Their contribution is meaningful and significant.

With the disappearance of money as a means of exchange, many crimes will disappear. As religions disappear, with their repressive superstitions and moralities, crimes like rape will become unheard of. And when from the very beginning every child is brought up with a reverence for life – reverence for the trees because they are alive, reverence for animals, reverence for birds – do you think such a child one day can be a murderer? It will be almost inconceivable.

And if life is joyous, full of songs and dances, do you think somebody will want to commit suicide? Ninety percent of crimes will disappear automatically; only ten percent of crimes may remain, which are genetic, which need hospitalization – but not jails, prisons, not people to be sentenced to death. This is all so ugly, so inhuman, so insane.

The new commune, the new man, can live without any law, without any order. Love will be his law, understanding will be his order. Science will be, in every difficult situation, his last resort.

Science in Service of Life

Are scientists now of the same category as politicians? In a way, yes. The politician is one whose whole desire is to have power; hence anybody whose desire is to have power, particularly over others – they may be human beings or material objects, it makes no difference. The politician is struggling to have power over people, the scientist is struggling to have power over matter, but the desire is the same and the mind is the same. So, in one way, they both are in the same boat. But there are many other ways in which science is totally different from politics.

Politics enslaves living people; hence it is more violent. Science tries to conquer matter; it is not a violent search. But science has grown to such complexity that now it is not possible for individual scientists to work on their own; they need immense support from politicians. Their research projects are so expensive that only governments of very rich nations can afford them. So the scientist unwittingly has fallen into the hands of the politicians. Now the scientist works as a servant to nationalism, to communism, to fascism, to capitalism. He is no longer an independent seeker; he is part of a certain political ideology. He works and discovers, but he has no control over his own discoveries; the control is in the hands of the politicians. They decide in which direction he should work; otherwise they will not financially support any other kind of project – and the politician's only project is war. So thousands of scientists of immense intelligence, talent and genius have become just slaves of a political mechanism that exploits their intelligence in the service of war and death.

Science can be of great importance if two things are added to it: one is that it should not only be an objective search, it should also open the subjective doors of consciousness. The scientist should not go on working only on objects; he has to work upon the scientist himself. Up to now the scientist has been denying his own consciousness. It is such an absurd attitude, so illogical and so unscientific, that it brings scientists closer to superstitious so-called religions. These religions believe blindly in a God they know nothing about, and the scientist goes on disbelieving in himself. This is also a form of superstition --enormous, unbelievable. If there is nobody inside you, if there is no consciousness in you, then who is going to discover the mysteries and secrets of matter, nature, and life? At this point, science has been behaving in an old and superstitious way; it has been imitating the religions.

I have been in contact with many professors of science and not a single one of them was able to give any argument in support of this superstition. They simply go on repeating that consciousness is only a by-product of matter. Whenever I have asked them, "On what grounds are you saying it? Who is the scientist who has proved it? Which are the discoveries that have been made to support the idea?" they have no answer. It is just because a man who was not a scientist at all, who was an economist, Karl Marx, created this idea that consciousness is only a by-product of matter.

Marx wanted to deny God and he wanted to deny the soul; his approach was philosophical. It can be understood if in the Soviet Union the scientists were repeating the same as Karl Marx, because to say anything against Karl Marx was to go against the holy scripture of communism. It was the same as in a fanatic Christian society, where you cannot say anything against the Bible. You may be right, that does not matter; it is not a question of being right or wrong. The Holy Bible cannot be contradicted; it is unforgivable sin. But the same was the situation in the Soviet Union as far as Karl Marx and his book *Das Kapital* was concerned.

But in a world where people are pretending to have the right of freedom of expression, the scientists go on repeating this superstition that consciousness is only a by-product of matter, without any understanding that Karl Marx was not a scientist and his statement is not based on any experiments.

Karl Marx was an atheist. Just as there are people who believe in God without knowing anything about God, there are people who do not believe in God without knowing anything about God. They don't differ basically; their quality is the same.

So in one aspect the scientist behaves like a fanatic, fundamentalist Christian. He goes on denying consciousness. And unless science opens up the dimension of the scientist's own interiority, it will not become a whole, comprehensive subject. It will remain partial; its viewpoint will remain only half of the truth.

You should remember that a whole lie is better than half a truth. The whole lie will be detected soon; the half-truth is very dangerous because it has something of truth in it. It can keep people in darkness for centuries. And three centuries have already passed for scientists. They have been working but they have not dared to inquire into the innermost being of man – that is one thing that has to be added to science; then it can become of tremendous importance.

To add subjectivity to objective science means adding the methods of meditation to the methods of concentration. The methods of concentration take you out, they are extrovert. Science requires a mind that has the capacity to concentrate. Meditation requires the capacity to go beyond mind, to go into silence, to be absolutely a pure nothingness.

Unless science accepts meditation as a valid method of enquiry it will remain a halfhearted search – and because of its halfheartedness, it is dangerous. It can easily serve the purposes of death because it does not believe in consciousness, it believes in dead matter, so it does not matter whether Nagasaki or Hiroshima happens, or even if the whole globe commits suicide. It doesn't matter, because all is matter. There is no consciousness; nothing is lost.

The scientist will revolt against the politicians only when the dimension of meditation is added in his research, in his work.

Secondly, the scientist has to realize now that he is providing the politicians with self-destructive weapons and technologies. He is behaving against humanity, he is behaving against the new humanity; he is behaving against his own children. He is sowing seeds of death for all. It is time that scientists should learn to discriminate: what helps life and what destroys life? Just for the sake of their salaries and comforts they should not go on like slaves and robots working for war and a destruction which is unprecedented.

The scientist has to be a revolutionary too. He has to be a spiritual seeker first, and second he has to be a revolutionary. And he has to remember not to serve death, whatsoever the cost. He has not to follow the directions of politicians. He has to decide himself what is helpful to the whole cosmos, what is helpful to the ecology, what is helpful to a better life, to a more beautiful existence. And he has to condemn the politicians if they force him to work in the service of death. He has to refuse totally, everywhere, in Russia, in America, in China, in every country all over the world.

Scientists need a global association of their own which can decide what research should be taken in hand and what research should be dropped.

Up to now science has been accidental. People have been just groping in the dark, finding something and becoming great discoverers. Now that time is over. Groping in the dark they have found atom bombs, nuclear weapons; they have done a great service!

Now it is their responsibility to destroy all the nuclear weapons, even though it goes against your so-called nationalism, your so-called communism, your so-called democracy. Nothing matters, because now even the very existence of man is at stake. Just as one day scientists revolted against religion and its dictates, now they have to revolt again against the politicians and their dictates.

The scientist has to stand on his own and be absolutely clear that he is not being exploited. Now he is being exploited everywhere. Just because he is being paid great salaries, given Nobel prizes, honors, he is ready to sacrifice the whole of humanity – for his Nobel prizes, for all those stupid awards. Scientists should no longer behave like children. These awards and prizes and these respectable posts are all toys to befool people, and even your great scientists are behaving like fools.

I would like my people to create an uproar all over the world against scientists who are serving governments and politicians in creating weapons for war. The masses have to be awakened against these scientists; they have become now the greatest danger, and their association with politicians has to be broken.

Science in itself can become both: accepting meditation it can become religion; being rebellious it can create a better life, more affluent, more abundant. It can be the greatest blessing to mankind – outwardly and inwardly. But right now it is one of the greatest dangers.

Most scientists are not at all aware of the new possibilities for a new world. They cannot be; they are in the service of the old approaches and the old humanity, the old politicians, the old ideologies. In fact they are preparing a funeral for the new. They should prepare a funeral for the old, which is already dead! And we are carrying its corpse – it stinks, but we have become immune because we have been born in a society which has been carrying corpses. We have grown up in a society, in educational institutions where everywhere corpses are worshiped.

If there is life anywhere on another planet – and scientists suspect that there is life on at least fifty thousand planets in the whole universe, and there may be planets where science has grown to far higher reaches – they may be able to observe our behavior. And they will be simply surprised: what are our geniuses doing? It would have been better if there were more idiots and fewer geniuses – at least life would have continued. These geniuses are going to destroy the whole of life.

The new can be accepted only if scientists understand that the world does not consist only of dead objects, it also consists of living beings – and not only of living beings but beings who are conscious too. And there is a possibility of growing this consciousness to great peaks. A Gautam Buddha and a Zarathustra are like Everest, Himalayan peaks. They show, they indicate the potential of every human being; just a little effort and you can also reach their heights. You can also reach the sunlit peaks; you need not live always in the dark caves, in the valleys of misery.

The dark night need not remain forever. There is a possibility to come out of the dark night into a beautiful morning with birds singing and flowers blossoming.

The scientists need a great incentive for meditation. Only then will they be able to see that what they have been doing is against the future of mankind. They are destroying the very hope…while with the same intelligence they could have created a paradise on earth, for their children and their children's children to live in a better world, with more health, with more love, with more consciousness.

Science has to become religious, it has to become spiritual. It has not to exhaust all its energies on the outer world but has to penetrate into the treasures of our inner being. It has great potential, but that potential is not yet used. Just as it has been successful in penetrating into the very secret of matter, it has the capacity to penetrate into the very secret of consciousness too. Then it will be a great blessing, a great benediction.

As far as my vision for a new humanity is concerned, I see science as having two dimensions: one, the lower dimension, working on objects; and two, the higher dimension, working on consciousness. And the lower dimension has to work as a servant to the higher dimension. Then there is no need of any other religion; then science fulfills totally all the needs of man.

But right now science transforms nothing. It cannot. Unless it approaches consciousness and works out how to develop more consciousness in man – how to make his unconscious conscious, how to transform his darkness into a noontide – it will not be of any great use. On the contrary, it is proving to be one of the greatest dangers.

It was Albert Einstein who wrote a letter before the second world war to President Roosevelt of America saying, "I can create atomic energy and atom bombs, and if you don't have atom bombs I can predict that it is impossible to win against Germany in the war." Einstein was a German Jew. He was working in Germany, researching for the German government, which was under the control of Adolf Hitler, to create an atom bomb. Just the very idea…if he had not been a Jew, the whole history of the world would have been totally different. If Germany could have produced atom bombs, then there would have been no power strong enough – neither America nor the Soviet Union nor England – to stand in the way of Adolf Hitler; he would have conquered the whole world.

But because Albert Einstein was a Jew…he was so important that he was not harassed by Adolf Hitler and his people, but he was seeing that millions of Jews were disappearing, in the gas chambers of the Nazi government. He would not have been killed because he was so much needed and there was nobody else to replace him, but he became afraid that if Adolf Hitler wins, then all over the world there will not be a single Jew left alive. He was not afraid about his own life; it was safe, because Adolf Hitler needed him.

Einstein escaped from Germany, leaving the experiment incomplete. The German scientists did everything they could, but there was no other Albert Einstein to complete the experiment. And Einstein wrote a letter to the enemy of Germany, to America, saying "I have escaped from Germany and I am ready to make atom bombs for America. Without atom bombs you cannot defeat Germany. And there is also a fear that somebody may be able to complete the experiment that I have left incomplete, because there were many scientists working with me, under me." Roosevelt immediately invited him and gave him all the facilities possible.

Truman was president at the time when the atom bombs were produced by Albert Einstein, and Einstein told Truman, "Now there is no need to use them, because Germany has committed a historical mistake."

This historical mistake has been committed many times. Anybody who wants to fight with Russia and has committed this historical mistake is doomed, because for nine months the whole country is covered with snow. Russia is so vast – it covers two continents, from one corner of Europe to the other corner of Asia. And there are only three months when the weather is clear enough to fight. And Russia has always had a big enough army to hold out against the enemy for three months and then wait for the winter. Winter lasts for nine months. Then Russia need not fight; that winter finishes the enemies without any trouble! Nobody can survive the Russian winter, except Russians – it needs a lifelong training. Napoleon got lost, in the first world war. Germany got lost, because Adolf Hitler again committed the same mistake.

But this time Truman did not even answer the letter of Albert

Einstein. The first letter was received with such great joy and he was invited with great welcome, was given all the resources he needed, but now the bombs were already in the hands of the politicians. Who cares about Albert Einstein? And he was saying simply, "Now there is no need. Germany is finished, and within two weeks at the most, Japan will be finished, because Japan cannot stand on its own. There is no need to use these bombs."

But Truman was in a hurry to use the atom bomb, because Germany had surrendered and if Japan should also surrender then there would be no opportunity to see what great power America had, and no opportunity to show the whole world.

Nagasaki and Hiroshima were destroyed unnecessarily. Japan was ready to surrender. Preparations were being done for how the surrender should happen; negotiations were going on between the generals. But Truman ordered, "Before the surrender at least we should demonstrate how much power we have. Once the war ends we won't have any opportunity." Two hundred thousand people in two great cities died within ten minutes – and not only people but trees, animals, birds, everything alive suddenly became dead.

Einstein was so shocked that before his death when somebody asked him, "If you are born again, would you like to be a physicist in your new life?" he said, "Never! If I am born again, I would rather be a plumber than a physicist. Enough is enough. I have seen how I worked day in, day out to create the atomic weapons. They were for an emergency, but once they were created I had no power over them. I had created them, but once they were created, the politicians had the keys in their hands. And my letter was not even answered! I am dying one of the most frustrated men on the earth."

He was one of the most successful men, perhaps the greatest scientist that we have ever known, but his own feeling was far more true. He was a man of conscience; he died almost like a wounded lion, utterly frustrated with politicians and their ugliness, their murderous and criminal minds.

Up to now, science certainly has not brought much of a transformation as far as human consciousness is concerned, but it has the potential – just a great awakening is needed.

The scientist has to realize his responsibility. He has almost become a god; either he can create or he can destroy. He has to be reminded that he is no longer the old scientist of the times of Galileo, just working in his own house, with a few tubes and a few bottles, just mixing chemicals and experimenting. Those days are gone. Now he has the power to destroy the whole life of this planet or to create a life so beautiful and so blissful that man has imagined it only in heaven; it can be possible here. A few small groups of scientists have started working on those lines. Nobody believes them.

For example, Japan created an artificial island – because in Japan there is such a shortage of land that it is becoming impossible to expand industries. Japan has become one of the richest countries in the world, and it needs more and more land. The old way was to conquer some other country; that is not possible anymore. The fear of a third world war hangs over everybody. So Japan created an artificial island to be used for industrial development. Once it becomes a success, many more artificial islands and Japan will be creating more earth than God created in those six days!

There are tremendous possibilities for science. Once it no longer serves death, it can float cities in the ocean. Japan has also tried to make underground cities, because why go on with the old conception that you have to live overground? You can live underground; it is more peaceful there, and you can get the right kind of light, the right kind of oxygen, because everything will be in the hands of the scientist. Just as underground cities are possible, floating cities in the ocean are possible, under the ocean cities are possible, flying cities are possible....

Once science changes its attitude and stops being supportive to politicians for war, so much energy will be released that scientists can do all these things which may appear off the wall to you, but they don't appear off the wall to me.

Science has great possibilities, but we have not yet been able to use those possibilities. And all the scientists are in the service of politicians, of governments – that means in the service of death and war. A great revolution is needed.

Just as scientists revolted once against religion, fought against religion, now they have to fight against politics, against nationalism.

Their responsibility is great. They are the most important people for the survival of humanity.

Do you see experiments on human life, such as artificial birth and the exchange of hearts and brains, as an advance, or as an action against nature?

It all depends who is going to do it. If the politicians are going to do it, or the so-called religions are going to do it, then it is against nature. They cannot do anything natural, they are against nature. But if it is being done by an international academy of scientists – I say *international* academy of scientists – it can be a tremendous, progressive step, and it will not be against nature. It will be nature's growth.

But it all depends on who is doing it. The experiments themselves are neutral. No experiment has any vested interest, it is neutral. You can use poison to kill you; the same poison can be used by medical people to save you. It all depends who is doing it.

For example, the discovery of atomic energy was a step of tremendously great progress, a quantum leap. We had found a key to transform the earth into paradise – so much energy in such a small atom. And they are in everything...just in a dewdrop there are millions of atoms. Any atom, if it is exploded, releases so much energy that you can make the whole earth live in luxury. Or you can create Hiroshima and Nagasaki – thousands of people dead within seconds.

But scientific progress falls into the hands of the politicians because only they can provide enough finance to make these discoveries possible. The scientists of the whole world should think it over: their genius is being used by idiots! The scientists should disconnect themselves from any nation, regardless of what country they live in. They should create an international academy of sciences. And it is not difficult. If all the scientists of the world are together, finances can be made available, and these discoveries can help man tremendously.

The international academy of scientists can be given every possible support. But they should be the decisive factors in what is going to happen through their experiments. And it is time the scientists should recognize their great responsibility. If a third world war happens then the scientists will be the greatest criminals, because they supplied all kinds of inventions to the politicians.

Science should not be the monopoly of any nation, any country. The whole idea is stupid. How can science be monopolized? And every country is trying to monopolize the scientists, keep their inventions secret. This is against humanity, against nature, against existence. Whatever a genius discovers should be in the service of the whole.

You are asking whether discoveries like changing human hearts or human brains are progressive steps. They are of great importance to bring a new humanity on the earth. If Einstein's body is no longer capable of living, do you think it would not be good if his whole brain could be transplanted into a young, healthy man? This way bodies may go on changing, but we can keep the genius of Albert Einstein growing for centuries. And if a man in a seventy-year life can give so much, you can imagine if his brain continues for centuries how much benefit it will be for humanity, for the whole universe.

As it is now, it is really a wastage: the container gets rotten, and you throw the content also. The body is only a container. If the container has become dirty, old, unusable, change the container, but don't throw away the content. The genius mind can live for eternity in different bodies; that is nothing against nature.

Your heart, if it starts failing, and if you are of immense value to humanity…what is the fear of exchanging the heart? Somebody may be dying from cancer, but his heart is perfectly healthy; that heart can be planted in a person who is talented, a genius, and is healthy otherwise, but the heart is not strong. This is simple; there is nothing in it against nature.

But with politicians and the power in their hands, of course every advance has gone against nature. Everything that human genius has discovered, invented, finally is in the service of death. So are the priests. Now science is no longer a child, that it has to depend on others. Science is now grown-up enough, it is adult. Just a little courage is needed.

It will be a great revolution in the history of man. The whole power will be in the hands of the scientists, who have never done any harm to anybody. And once all the power is in the hands of the scientists, politicians will fade away of their own accord. They have been exploiting scientists for their own purposes, and to be exploited by anybody is not an act of dignity.

The scientists should recognize their dignity, they should recognize their individuality. They should recognize that they have been exploited down the ages by the priests and the politicians. Now it is time to declare that science is going to stand on its own feet. This will be a great freedom.

Then all these experiments, such as laboratory babies, will be of a different caliber, because you can arrange what kind of genius you want. Up to now it has been just accidental, and because it has been accidental, ninety-nine percent of the people have nothing to contribute. They contribute only problems to the world. What have the poor countries contributed to the world – or even the rich countries? Except problems, wars, there is no contribution on their part.

But if you can give birth to a child in a scientific lab… It is possible, there is no problem in it. The male semen and the woman's egg can meet in a tube. There is no need to go on in the old bullock cart way. We can look and we can have the whole picture of what this child is going to be. If we want more poets, we can create more poets. If we want more musicians, we can create more musicians. And we can create only geniuses; there is no need for mediocre people – they have had their day.

We can give the child strength, long life. We can make sure that he never becomes sick, that he will never becomes old. It is just a question of managing and finding the right egg and the right male contribution to the egg. What we have been doing is just utterly unintelligent.

And this will free man also from guilt, possessiveness, jealousy, because you will not be producing children. Sex, for the first time, will be simply fun! Children will be produced in the lab. They will belong to all. And because you are not going to produce children in the old way, then many problems of your life will be simply dissolved.

Why is the man so insistent…? Throughout the ages the insistence has remained there: he wants to be certain that the child born out of his wife's womb is his. Why? Who are you anyway? It is a question of property, because your child will become the inheritor of all that you have accumulated. You want to be certain that it is your child, not your neighbor's child. Women have been kept almost imprisoned, for the simple fear that if they start mixing with people it will be difficult to decide whose child it is. Only the mother will know, or even she may not know.

Once production of life goes into the hands of science, sex will be transformed. Then you are not jealous, then you are not a monopolist, then monogamy is absurd. Then sex is just fun, the way you enjoy tennis. And you don't bother that the partners should remain monogamous – two bodies enjoying each other… And there will be no fear that the wife may get pregnant and there will be problems, financial and other.

Sex will no longer be a problem for the world population; it will no longer be a problem for the priest. In fact, if children are produced in the scientific lab, many of the troubles of the world will dissolve. And we can create the best people: beautiful, healthy, capable of living as long as we want. Old age is not necessary – a man can remain young, healthy, without sickness.

All these hospitals and so many people, so much money involved… Do you know? America spends more money on laxatives than on education. Great idea! Who cares about education? The question is laxatives!

But the basic thing should be remembered. Scientists have to be courageous enough and declare that they don't belong to any nation, to any religion, that whatsoever they will be doing will be for the whole humanity. And I don't see that there is anything impossible in it.

I am absolutely for those progressive inventions which can make man happier, live longer, be younger, healthier, and which make his life more of a play, fun, and less of a torturous journey from the cradle to the grave.

I heard you speak of scientists choosing future people from their genetic analysis of sperms. I have no trust in scientists, or doctors or anybody whose knowledge extends no further than their head. I intuitively feel that genetics plays only a small role in determining what a person becomes. A gardener may well have become a musician; a soldier may have the potential to be a scientist. Surely what a man is, is no measure of what he might have been in different circumstances.

Please speak more on the underlying sanity behind your suggestion – which I cannot see because of my fear of totalitarian regimes.

I can understand your concern; it is my concern too. But there are many things to be understood. The first is, never act out of fear. If man had acted out of fear there would have been no progress possible.

For example, the people who invented bicycles…can you ever think of any danger? It is simply inconceivable that bicycles can be dangerous. But then the Wright brothers made the first flying machine out of the parts of bicycles. The whole world rejoiced – nobody could have foreseen that airplanes would be used to destroy cities, millions of people, in the Second World War.

But the same airplanes are also carrying millions of people around the world. They have made the world small, they have made it possible to call the world just a global village. They have made bridges between peoples, they have brought together people of different races, religions, languages in a way that no other invention had been able to do before. So the first thing to remember is that acting out of fear is not the right way.

Act cautiously, with consciousness, remembering the possibilities and the dangers, and creating the atmosphere to prevent those dangers. Now, what can be more dangerous than nuclear weapons in the hands of the politicians? You have put the most dangerous thing into their hands.

Now, in fact there is no need to be afraid; even nuclear weapons can be used creatively. And I have a deep trust in life, that they will eventually be used creatively. Life cannot allow itself to be destroyed so easily, it is going to give tremendous resistance. In that resistance is hidden the birth of a new man, of a new dawn, of a new order, of the whole of life and existence.

According to me, nuclear weapons have made a great war impossible. Gautam Buddha could not do it, Jesus Christ could not do it. All the saints of the world together have been talking about nonviolence, no war; they could not succeed. But nuclear weapons have done their job. Seeing that the danger is so great, all the politicians are trembling deep down, that if a third world war begins the whole of life will be destroyed – and they will be included in it. They cannot save themselves. Nothing can be saved. This is a great chance for all those who love creation. This is the moment when we can turn the whole trend of science towards creativity.

Remember one thing – science is neutral. It simply gives you power. Now, how to use it depends on you, depends on the whole of humanity and its intelligence. Science gives us more power to create a better life, to create more comfortable living, to create more healthy human beings – rather than preventing...just out of fear that some totalitarian power may misuse it.

Everything can be misused. And the questioner himself is a doctor; he himself belongs to the category of scientists. He should understand one thing, that everything that can harm can also be of tremendous benefit. Don't condemn anything, just raise the consciousness of human beings.

Communal and Individual – New Forms of Living Together

In the whole of existence, only man needs rules. No other animal needs any rules.

The first thing that has to be understood is that there is something artificial about rules. The reason man needs them is that he has left being an animal, and yet he has not become human; he is in a limbo. That is the source of the need for all the rules. If he were an animal, there would be no need. Animals live perfectly well without any rules, constitutions, laws, courts. If man really becomes human, not just in name but in reality...

Very few people have realized that up to now. For example, for men like Socrates, Zarathustra, Bodhidharma, there is no need of any rules. They are alert enough not to do any harm to anybody. There is no need for any laws, for any constitutions. If the whole society evolves to be authentically human, there will be love but there will not be law.

The problem is that man needed rules, laws, governments, courts, armies, police force, because he lost his natural behavior of being an animal and he has not yet regained another natural status. He is just in between. He is nowhere, he is a chaos. To control that chaos all these things like rules and laws are needed.

The problem becomes more complex, because the forces that were evolved to control man – religions, states, courts – became so powerful. They had to be given power; otherwise how would they exercise control? So we fell into slavery on our own. Now that they have become powerful that they don't want to drop their vested interests. They don't want man to evolve.

When you ask how the individual and the society can evolve, you do not understand the problem. If the individual evolves, society dissolves. The society exists only because the individual is not allowed to evolve. All these powers have for centuries been controlling man, and enjoying their power and their prestige. They are not ready to let man evolve, to let man grow to a point where they become useless.

The forces that we created to keep man from falling apart into chaos – the military leaders, the lawmakers, the courts, the religious leaders – are now so powerful that they don't want to leave you free to grow. If you are capable of growing, becoming an individual, alert, aware and conscious, there will be no need of all these people. They will lose their jobs, and with their jobs they will lose their prestige, their power, their leadership, their priesthood, their popehood; everything will be gone. So now, those who were in the beginning needed for protection have turned into the enemies of humanity.

My approach is not to fight against these people – they are powerful, they have armies, they have money, they have everything. You cannot fight with them, you will be destroyed. The only way out of this mess is to silently start growing your own consciousness, which they cannot prevent by any force. In fact they cannot even know what is going on inside you.

I offer you the alchemy of inner transformation. Change your inner being. And the moment you are changed, completely transformed, you will suddenly see you are out of the imprisonment, you are no longer a slave. You were a slave because of your chaotic state.

It happened in the Russian revolution... The day the revolution succeeded, one woman started walking in Moscow in the middle of the road. The policeman said, "This is not right. You cannot walk in the middle of the road."

The woman said, "Now we are free." But even if you are free, you will have to follow the rules of traffic; otherwise traffic will become impossible. If cars and people are running everywhere they want, turning wherever they want, don't take any note of the lights, people will be simply getting into accidents and being killed. This will bring the army in, to enforce the law that you have to walk to the right or to the left, whichever is chosen by the country – but nobody can walk in the middle. Then at the point of a gun you have to follow the rules. I always remember that woman; she is very symbolic.

Freedom does not mean chaos. Freedom means more responsibility, so much responsibility that nobody need interfere in your life. That you can be left alone, that the government need not interfere with you, that the police need not interfere with you, that the law has nothing to do with you – you are simply outside of their world.

This is my approach if you really want to transform humanity: each individual should start growing on his own. And in fact a crowd is not needed for growth. Growth is something like a child growing in a mother's womb: no crowd is needed; the mother has just to be careful.

A new man has to be born in you. You have to become the womb of a new man. Nobody will come to know about it, and it is better that nobody knows about it. You simply go on doing your ordinary work, living in the ordinary world, being simple and ordinary – not becoming revolutionaries, reactionaries, punks and skinheads. That is not going to help. That is sheer stupidity. It is out of frustration, I understand, but still it is insane. The society is insane and out of frustration you become insane.

The society is not afraid of those people; the society is afraid only of people who can become so centered, so conscious that laws become useless for them. They always do right; they are beyond the grip of the so-called powerful interests.

If individuals grow, society will diminish. The way we have known society – with the government, with the army, with the courts, with the policemen, with the jails – this society will diminish.

Certainly, because there are so many human beings, new forms of collectivities will come into being. I would not like to call them "society," just to avoid the confusion between the words. I call the new collectivity a commune. The word is significant: it means a place where people are not only living together, but where people are in deep communion.

To live together is one thing; we are doing it: in every city, every town, thousands of people are living together – but what togetherness is there? People don't even know their neighbors. They live in the same skyscraper, hundreds of people, and they never come to know that they are living in the same house. It is not togetherness, because there is no communion. It is simply a crowd, not a community. So I would like to replace the word "society" with the word "commune."

Society has existed on certain basic principles. You will have to remove them, otherwise the society will not disappear. The first and the most important unit of society has been the family: if the family remains the way it is, then the society cannot disappear. Then the church cannot disappear, then religions cannot disappear. Then we cannot create one world, one humanity.

The family is psychologically out of date. It is not that it was always there; there was a time when there was no family, people lived in tribes. The family came into existence because of private property. There were powerful people who managed to have more private property than anybody else, and they wanted it to be given to their children. Up to that point there was no problem. Men and women were meeting out of love; there was no marriage and no family. But once property came into existence, the man became very possessive of the woman. He turned the woman also into part of his property.

In Indian languages the woman is called "property." In China the woman became so much like property that even if a husband killed his wife there was no law against it. No crime was committed – you are absolutely free to destroy your own property. You can burn your furniture, you can burn your house. It is not a crime, it is your house. You can kill your wife.

With private property the woman also became private property, and every strategy was used so that the man could be absolutely certain that the child that was born from his wife was really his own. Now, this is a difficult problem: the father can never be absolutely certain; only the mother knows. But the father created every kind of barrier to the woman's freedom of movement so that she could not come into contact with other men. All possibilities and all doors were closed.

It is not a coincidence that only old women go to your churches and temples, because that is the only place they were allowed to go throughout history, knowing perfectly well that the church is protective of the family. The church knows perfectly well that once the family is gone the church is gone. And the church, of course, is the last place where some romantic affair could happen. They have made every precaution: the priest has to be celibate…. These are guarantees – the priest is celibate, he is against sex, he is against women. It is expressed in different religions in different ways.

The Jaina monk cannot touch a woman; in fact the woman should not come closer than eight feet to the Jaina monk. The Buddhist monk is not allowed to touch a woman. There are religions that don't allow women to enter into their religious temples, or they have separating partitions – the man has the main part and the woman has a small corner, but separated. The men cannot even see them; meeting is impossible.

Many religions, like Mohammedanism, have covered their women's faces. Mohammedan women's faces have become pale because they never see the sunlight. Their whole body is covered; their face is covered. The woman is not to be educated, because education gives people strange kinds of thoughts. People start thinking, people start arguing. The woman was not allowed to have any paid career, because that means independence. So she was cut off from every angle, just so that you the man can be certain that his son is really his son. Those who were really powerful – for example kings – had male servants castrated, because they were moving throughout the palace, working and serving. They had to be castrated; otherwise, there was a danger.

And there was danger, because every emperor had hundreds of wives, many of whom he would never see. Naturally they could fall in love with anybody. So only castrated men were allowed into the palace. In that way, even if they fell in love they could not create children. That was the basic concern.

The family has to disappear and give place to the commune. A commune means that we have pooled all our energies, all our money, everything into a single pool – which will be taking care of all the people. The children will belong to the commune, so there is no question of individual heritage.

And it is so economical... I have seen in my commune in America: 5000 people were there; that means 2500 kitchens would have been needed if they were living separately and 2500 women would be wasting their lives in the kitchen.

There was only one kitchen for 5000 people, and only fifteen people were running it. And remember, every woman is not a good cook! In fact, the best cooks are always men. All the best books on cookery are written by men, and in all the great hotels you will find the best cooks are men. Two thousand five hundred people cannot afford the best cooks separately, but a 5000-person commune can afford the best cooks, the best food. It can afford doctors to look into whether what they are eating is junk or food – most people are eating junk. To be right, the food has to be medically decided. In my commune fifteen people were preparing the food, doctors were looking at its hygiene, its cleanliness and its nutritious value. It is nutrition that should be valued. Flavor is a small thing; that can be given to any kind of food, good flavor. You need not eat junk just for flavor – and if you eat junk, sooner or later you are going to become junk. There are so many junkies all around! If you look in their heads you will find ice cream and nothing else...spaghetti!

You need a proportionate, calculated food balance to keep all your needs completely fulfilled. Food that helps consciousness to grow, food that makes you more loving, more peaceful, food that destroys your anger, your hatred. It is your chemistry that food changes, and all these things – anger, hatred, love, compassion – are connected with your chemistry. There should be a chemist to look at what kind of food is being given to people.

If you pool all your energies, all your money and all your resources, every commune can be rich and every commune can enjoy being alive.

Once individuals are growing and communes are growing side by side, society will disappear, and with society all the evils that the society has created.

I will give you one example. Only in China was a tremendously revolutionary step taken two thousand years ago. This was that the doctor had to be paid by the patient only as long as the patient remained healthy. If he fell sick, then the doctor had not to be paid. That looks very strange. We pay the doctor when we are sick, and he makes us healthy again. But this is dangerous, because you are making the doctor dependent on your sickness. Sickness becomes his interest: the more people fall sick, the more he can earn. His interest becomes not health, but sickness. If everybody remains healthy, then the doctor will be the only one who will be sick!

They came up with a revolutionary idea, practical, that every person should have his physician, and as long as he remains healthy he has to pay the doctor every month. It is the duty of the doctor to keep him healthy – and naturally he will keep him healthy because he is being paid for it. If the person falls sick, the doctor loses money. When there are epidemics the doctor goes bankrupt.

Right now it is just the opposite.

The doctor – I have heard the story – came to Mulla Nasruddin and said, "You have not paid and I have been again and again coming and reminding you that I cured your child of smallpox, and you don't listen."

Mulla said, "You had better listen to me! Otherwise I am going to sue you in the court."

The doctor said, "This is strange…I treated your child."

He said, "Yes, that I know – but who spread the epidemic through the whole town? Your child – and all the money you have earned from that epidemic you have to divide with me."

Nasruddin was right. The doctor's child had done a great job, and after that day the doctor never came back again to ask for the money for the treatment that he had given to Mulla Nasruddin's child. Mulla's argument was correct. The doctor had earned enough out of the epidemic already.

But this is a very wrong system. The commune should pay the doctor to keep the commune healthy, and if anybody gets sick in the commune the doctor's salary is cut. In this way, health is the business of the doctor – not sickness. And you can see the difference. In the West the doctor's business is called "medicine," which relates to sickness. In the East it is called "ayurveda," which means the science of life, not of sickness.

The basic business of the doctor should be that people should live long, should live healthy, whole, and he should be paid for it. So each commune can afford very easily to keep the doctor, the plumber, the engineer – whatever is needed. That is the commune's responsibility to take care of .

The people who serve the commune should be rotating, so there is no power arising again. The committee of the commune should be in rotation; every year new people are coming in and old people are going out, so nobody becomes addicted to power. Power is the worst drug that people can become addicted to; it should be given, but in very small doses and not for a long time. Let the individual grow and let the commune grow – and forget all about society; don't fight with it. Don't even say, "We are creating an alternative society."

We have nothing to do with society; let society go on as it is. If it wants to live it will have to change its mode, its form, its structure, and it will have to become a commune. If it wants to die, let it die. There is no harm. The world is overpopulated; it needs only one-fourth of its population. So the old rotten heads who cannot conceive of anything new, who are absolutely blind and cannot see that what they are doing is harmful and poisonous…if they have decided to die, then let them die silently. Don't disturb them.

I don't teach you to be rebellious and to be revolutionaries. I want you to be very silent, almost underground transformers. Because all the revolutions have failed…now the only possible way is that we should do it so silently and so peacefully that it can happen.

There are things which happen only in silence. For example, if you love trees, you should not pull up the rose bush every day to look at its roots; otherwise you will kill it. Those roots have to remain hidden. Silently they go on doing their work.

Be just like roots: silently go on doing the work, changing yourself, changing anybody who is interested; spreading the methods that can change; creating small pools, small groups, small communes and wherever possible bigger communes. But let this whole thing happen very silently, without creating any upheaval.

> *You seem to be against communism as a valid form of social organization. Why is that?*

I am against communism, but for a strange reason. The reason is that it is not communism at all. The word communism is derived from "commune" – but communism is not commune-ism. It has no base in the idea of the commune; on the contrary, it is simply anticapitalism. Its name gives you the false notion of something positive, but in fact it is only a negative approach: it is anti-capitalism. And my understanding is that anything that is basically negative cannot help man's evolution in any way.

It is because of this fact that atheism has not been of any help to man's evolution, his consciousness, his growth. It is just pure negativity. Just saying that there is no God, and basing your whole philosophy on the belief in no-God, is sheer stupidity. Life needs something positive. In fact it needs something so positive that it can absorb the negative also, so powerfully positive that the negative need not be excluded from it; instead, it can be absorbed.

Jesus says, "Man cannot live by bread alone." I cannot agree with him, because mostly man lives by bread alone. Most human beings have lived by bread alone. I know what his implication was. I am not against his implication, I am against his statement. The implication is that man needs something more than the physical, something more than the bodily, something higher, transcendental, without which man can vegetate but cannot live. I support the implication, but Jesus' statement is very poor.

Why did I mention the statement? I want to make a similar statement but one with tremendous meaning. I say unto you that man cannot live by the negative alone. And communism is only a negative philosophy, like atheism.

Just think: How can you grow with no's surrounding you?

Growth needs the staircase of yes. No is dead; it is equivalent to death. Death is the ultimate no.

Life is the ultimate yes. Life needs the base of some yes-philosophy. Communism has nothing to offer.

Why is Karl Marx against capitalism? It is not that he is against capitalism; he is a poor man, and is full of jealousy against those who are rich. Three generations in Marx's family had been poor. He himself remained unemployed and poor his whole life. It is very strange: he was dependent on a rich friend, but writing against capitalism. The rich friend, Friedrich Engels, was a capitalist who owned factories. He had been feeding Karl Marx and his family his whole life, and Marx never worked for a single day; he earned not a single cent.

Engels must have been a man of great compassion. He could see the man had genius and needed support.

Although he was writing against capitalism, Marx was a great logician: he convinced Engels also that capitalism is the whole cause of all the problems in the world: "If we can destroy capitalism and distribute the wealth equally to people, all problems will disappear."

Karl Marx is basically a jealous man, rationalizing his jealousy into beautiful jargon. The remedy that he proposes is fallacious. Firstly, if you distribute the wealth of those who are rich to the poor, what will be the result? The poor will not become rich, the rich will only become poor: you will be distributing poverty. Yes, people will not feel jealous any more because they will all be equally poor.

I am against poverty, hence I am against communism. I want people to be equally rich, not equally poor. But for that a totally different approach is needed. It is not a question of distribution of wealth – because there is not much wealth to distribute. How many people are there who are rich? –perhaps two percent.

Now, the wealth of two percent distributed to ninety-eight percent of poor people is just like a spoonful of sugar thrown into the ocean to make it sweet. You are simply losing one spoonful of sugar unnecessarily. At least it could have given one man one cup of tea, and now even that is gone. Not that others are gaining anything, but they will all enjoy the idea: "Now nobody is drinking tea, we are all equal." Otherwise this man was drinking tea and everybody was jealous.

The people who have created wealth have a certain talent for creating it. You should use their talent; you should make it an art to be taught to everybody. They are not to be punished because they have created wealth.

In an aboriginal society, a primitive society, of which a few fragments are still alive here and there on the earth, nobody is poor and nobody is rich; of course there is no jealousy. Everybody owns nothing, everybody equally owns nothing; but nobody is producing wealth.

In fact the people who are producing wealth are creating an urge in others also to create wealth. Don't destroy these people – use these people as symbols. They have a certain art of creating wealth – make that art available to everybody, educate everybody. You teach economics in the universities; it would be far better if you taught the art of becoming rich – because by teaching economics you don't help them to know the art of becoming rich. They win gold medals in the universities and then they disappear.

When I was a professor I asked one of my vice-chancellors, "Have you ever thought about what happens to your gold medalists? They should shine in the society everywhere. What is the purpose of your gold medal? A man who stood first in the whole university disappears and is never heard about again. What happens to him? That shows simply the poverty of your gold medal and the poverty of all your education. Even if he made it to the top of your whole educational system, what has he gained?"

I have asked professors of economics, "You have been teaching economics for twenty or thirty years – how rich have you become?"

They said, "But what has that to do with teaching economics?"

I said, "Economics should be the science of becoming rich. You are just a poor professor, and if in thirty years of teaching you have not been able to find some secret of creating riches, what about your students? Have any of them become rich?" No, economics is not concerned about that; it is concerned about absolutely theoretical questions which have nothing to do with practical life.

Marx's idea is the distribution of wealth. Why? The reason he proposes is psychologically wrong, absolutely wrong. His reason is that every man is equal. That is psychologically absurd. What to say about all men, the whole humanity – not even two individuals are equal. Each individual is so unique, he cannot be equal to any other individual.

By saying that all human beings are equal Karl Marx is destroying the uniqueness of the individual. That's why I am against him and his whole philosophy – because I stand for the uniqueness of the individual. I am not saying that somebody is superior to you and somebody is inferior to you. Remember it! I am simply saying that you are not comparable to anybody:

You are you, and the other is the other. You don't compare a rose with a lotus, you simply say that they are two different things. Two different individuals, although they are both human beings, are unique individuals – incomparable.

Marx gives this idiotic idea – and it has been purchased by everybody all over the world: communists, anti-communists, everybody has purchased it; even the capitalists have purchased the idea that all men are equal. Why has nobody criticized it and fought it? For the simple reason that it looks very humanitarian. My God! Has something to be true or untrue – does its validity have to be judged by logic or by humanitarianism? Then any lie that appears to be humanistic has to be accepted. And upon that lie that all men are equal the whole structure of communism has been raised.

Now, you know, it is such a simple thing to understand – that every individual has different degrees of intelligence and different dimensions of creativity. Everybody cannot be a poet, everybody cannot be a scientist, everybody cannot be a painter. And it is good that everybody cannot be, otherwise life would lose all joy. The joy is in the uniqueness of the individual – that he is so unique, unrepeatable, irreplaceable, that once he is gone his place is going to remain empty forever. Nobody can fulfill his place; the way he was fulfilling it, only he could do it.

Marx takes away the whole dignity of the individual. And it is cunning, because he gives the idea of equality of all human beings. In such a beautiful idea of equality you will not be able to detect what he has taken away from you. He has made you just a cog in the wheel, replaceable. He has put you on the assembly line in a factory which produces cars, and the same car goes on being assembled automatically.

Ford produces a car every minute. Every minute, for twenty-four hours, a similar car goes on coming out of the assembly line. But man is not an assembled mechanism; you cannot take him apart and assemble him again. It would have been very helpful in a way if we could take a person apart – clean his insides and everything, replace a few bulbs here and there, a few fuses that have gone out, a few nuts and bolts that have got loose or too tight – and then assemble him again with a new battery. It would have been really good; but it would also be the greatest calamity that can happen. Then man disappears; then he is only a robot running on a battery. It is simple: if he breaks his hand there is no trouble, spare parts are always available. He just goes to any workshop and his hand is changed; he gets a brand-new hand – no problem.

Only once in a while he may have a problem when he is telling some woman, "I love you," and then he goes "Grrrr, grrr, grrrr...my battery is running out...just call the mechanic...." Only once in a while will he go "Grrrr, grrrr" – he won't be able to speak, the battery is running out. Or you may be supplied with a small meter which goes on showing you on your wrist what is going down, what is going up, what is needed now: if you need a little more petrol, or water, or the oil has to be changed. It will be simpler – but you will not be human, you will be robots.

Marx, by making you equal, is proposing a philosophy which ultimately is bound to make you robots – that is the Marxist philosophy's logical conclusion.

Only robots can be equal.

Man's dignity is in his uniqueness.

But let me repeat – because there is every possibility that I will be misunderstood – I am not saying that somebody is superior to you and somebody is inferior to you. I am simply saying that the very idea of comparison is invalid; you are just yourself. I cannot call you unequal, I cannot call you equal. Do you follow me? I cannot call you unequal.

That is the criticism communists have been throwing at me – that I am saying that people are unequal. That is absolutely unjust. I am not saying people are unequal, I am saying they are not equal; that implies they are not unequal either. The very idea of comparison is invalid. Man is unique. Man is not just a member of the society, a part of the society. He is an individual, an independent whole in himself .

Just think of it in this way and you will see it completely clearly:

if somebody says that everybody has to be writing poetry, then even if some people are writing better poetry than you, their poetry has to be distributed on an equal basis with yours. Everybody has to be equally a poet, equally a musician.

You can see the absurdity, that if Yehudi Menuhin has to be made equal to you, you won't gain anything, and that poor fellow will lose everything. You cannot be Yehudi Menuhin. He has a certain genius that is born with him, that is in his very chemistry, in his very physiology, in his very being. You don't have that chemistry, that physiology, that being. His parents were different, his parents' parents were different. You cannot have his quality distributed, that is impossible. And that will destroy all the beautiful flowers in human life. But you don't think that way. You think Yehudi Menuhin is just himself; there is no question of somebody else taking his qualities, dividing and distributing them.

What you don't understand is that in exactly the same way there are people who have a certain talent to be rich. Everybody is not Henry Ford, cannot be; and there is no need. One Henry Ford has created enough traffic, no need for more! If there are many Henry Fords then do you know what will be the result? The result will be that walking will be faster than driving. It is already becoming so. In cities like New York, Bombay, Tokyo and Calcutta, a distance you can cover by walking within ten minutes to fifteen minutes will take you an hour in a car.

I used to stay in Calcutta with one of the most significant, talented, rich men – Sahu Shantiprasad. Now he is dead. The auditorium where I used to give my talks and his house were only a ten-minute walk apart, but in his limousine it was unpredictable. If my lecture was going to be from seven-thirty, he would start panicking from five, telling me to get ready.

I said, "You are just mad! The lecture will start at seven-thirty and it is only a ten-minute walk. If we walk it will take ten minutes."

But he said, "We are not going to walk. And traffic in Calcutta is so chaotic that you never know… We have to leave here at least one and a half hours before." And sometimes it used to happen that we were still late, but sometimes we were too early and then we would just sit in the car. I said, "This is so stupid, Sahu Shantiprasad."

But he said, "I cannot allow you to walk – you are my guest."

I said, "That's true, I am your guest, but I have to sit in your car for four hours coming and going. This is strange, because in four hours I can reach Bombay or Delhi, but I only reach this poor auditorium!"

If there are many Henry Fords it will become a more difficult world than it is right now. No, nature produces enough people for any particular purpose. Nature has a very deep balancing power.

For example, when children are born, if a hundred girls are born today, then one hundred and ten boys will be born. About that data I was simply surprised. Why one hundred girls and one hundred and ten boys? Is nature also male chauvinistic? No, it is not that: nature is simply a balancing power. Ten boys die before a marriageable age. Girls are more resistant to diseases; boys are weaker as far as resistance to sickness is concerned. They may have muscular power – that is a different power – but as far as resistance to disease, sickness and death is concerned, they are less powerful than women.

So one hundred girls will suffice for one hundred and ten boys, because ten boys will be missing by the time they reach the marriageable age, something nature is balancing from the very beginning. Otherwise there will be ninety boys and one hundred girls. Those ten girls will be in difficulty, and will create so much difficulty for the ninety boys that you cannot conceive… It will be a chaos. Those ten girls without husbands, without boyfriends – do you think they are just going to sit and meditate? They will start grabbing hold of somebody else's husband, and then it is going to be a chaos. To avoid that chaos nature has to be alert from the very beginning to supply ten boys more, because they will be missing at the right time.

If nature is as balanced as that, it was balancing other things also till man started to interfere with it. For centuries the population of the world had remained the same. It was only man who started interfering with nature – through medicine, through new inventions to increase man's life span. Now you have created a trouble in the world. Nature was keeping the balance: people were born, but enough people were dying. It was almost always equal. What you have done is that you have prevented death, but you are not allowed to prevent birth. Now the pope goes on issuing sermons that abortions should be made illegal, that birth control should not be used.

In America when Ronald Regan was president, there was demonstration of seventy thousand people in the capital demanding that abortion should be declared illegal. When President Reagan – just look at these politicians! – was governor of California he had signed a bill for the legalization of abortion, because in California there was a great movement in favor of legalizing it. Then he signed the bill, but later he inaugurated a procession that wanted the constitution amended, and abortion declared illegal again because it is "against religion and against life." Reagan inaugurated that protest because all the orthodox people in the country were supporting this movement. When he spoke to that procession, Reagan said, "In my whole life I have committed only one mistake, and that was when I was governor of California and I signed that bill. That was the only mistake that I have committed."

Politicians can change their face very easily. Wherever the crowd is going, they jump ahead of it. They cannot lose, so they have to be very alert.

I have said many times that the political leaders are followers of their followers. The great politician is one who knows where the followers are going and keeps himself ahead of them. Wherever they are going does not matter; he should just remain ahead of them so they always know that he is the leader. He should keep his every sense alert, otherwise someday he will look back – and all the followers will have moved somewhere else; he will be standing alone. Now he will run and find the followers, and immediately try to get ahead of them again. What can he do? – he has to be the leader in every case. His business is to be the leader, it does not matter what the cause is. What do you want? It doesn't matter; all that matters is that he is ahead of you.

All these people – Catholics, Hindus, Mohammedans, Jews – who are against abortion and birth control should be a little logical about it. Then they should be against saving people's lives too; then there will be a balance. But nobody thinks of that.

There are people in the hospitals unnecessarily harassing the doctors and the nurses. Their legs are hanging up in one direction and their hands are hanging up in some other direction, another person needs the continual attendance of a doctor and a nurse, and so many medicines. And a person is on oxygen; if you just turn the oxygen off he will be gone. Why are you keeping him alive? What is the purpose of his being alive? Why are you torturing him? But the doctors have been taught that their purpose is to save life. That was taught by Hippocrates two thousand years ago when death was rampant.

Now these fools go on taking the oath of Hippocrates. Every medical student takes the oath of Hippocrates: "My whole life I will try to save life." But things have changed. When Hippocrates said that, out of ten children, nine were dying before they became two years of age; one was surviving. Of course the man was saying something meaningful when he told them to try to save life, but now the situation is just the reverse. Even in countries like India, out of ten children only one is dying. And every effort is being made to save that one, too.

One can understand trying to save a child; but why are you saving old people who have lived, lived enough, suffered, enjoyed, did all kinds of things, good and bad? Now it is time; let them go. But the doctors cannot let them go because it is illegal. They cannot put them off oxygen, so you go on saving the dying or almost-dead people. No pope issues a commandment that these people should be allowed freedom from their bodies. And what of their bodies is left? Somebody's heart is not working so a battery is working instead of the heart; somebody's lungs are not working; somebody's kidneys are not working, so mechanical kidneys are doing the work of the kidneys. But what is the purpose of these people? What will they do even if you continue to keep them going this way?

Yes, at the most they keep a few people employed, that's all. But what kind of a creative life are they going to have? What joy can they have in all that is being done to them? Continual injections are being given to them. They cannot sleep, then sleeping pills are given to them. They cannot wake up, then they are given medications so that they have to wake up. But for what reason, the Hippocratic oath? Let Hippocrates go to hell! He had no idea what his oath was going to bring about.

There should be some movement so that when people have lived enough and they desire to be freed from their bodies, then hospitals should provide a convenient, pleasant death. It is absolutely sane that every hospital should have a special ward with all facilities so that death becomes a pleasant experience, enjoyable.

Instead of medicines a meditator should be there to teach the dying man how to meditate, because now medicine is not needed, meditation is needed – how to relax and peacefully disappear from this body. Every hospital needs meditators – they are essential – just as it needs doctors. Up to now meditators were not needed because there was only one function: to save life. Now the function is doubled: to help people die. Every university should have a department where meditation is taught so that people themselves are ready. When the time comes to die, they are fully ready to die with joy, with celebration.

But assisted suicide is a crime. This will be considered assisted suicide and I will be considered to be teaching people illegal things. But what else can I do? I can say only what is absolutely right; whether it is legal or illegal I don't care a bit. My concern is with truth, not with law. The truth is that you have unbalanced life, nature. Please give back its balance. Either you have to stop saving children, and abortions should remain legal, birth control methods should be used widely … in fact it should be a crime not to use them. If somebody is caught not using them he should be jailed.

But it is a strange world: produce more children and you will have less income tax. A great world! The government is supporting you to have more children. What kind of logic is that? If I am to make the law, I will say the more children you have, the more income tax; with each child it is doubled. Have as many as you want but the income tax goes on being doubled each time – so even the rich cannot afford them, what to say about the poor and the middle class. Then only will they think of birth control; otherwise they are not going to.

The mind that Karl Marx had was certainly very talented. He created a worldwide movement – certainly he outdid Jesus. This is just Jewish competition. It is nobody's business really, just Jews competing. Freud created a worldwide movement for psychoanalysis, but Marx is on the top. Almost half the world is communist now – but not rich, very poor.

You can see how it worked in Germany. Just beyond the wall was the communist world. Of the same Berlin which was destroyed in the second world war, half remained free and democratic, and half was taken over by the communists. The half that remained independent, free and capitalist, grew rich: skyscrapers, beautiful roads, everything. It was as if the second world war had never happened. In the free West Berlin, the second world war left not even a trace; in fact the war had done something really good because all the old, dilapidated, rotten things finished and everything could be fresh and new. West Berlin became the most modern, youngest and freshest city in the whole world.

And on the other side it was dark and dismal, as if the second world war had just ended yesterday; people were living in dilapidated barracks. The whole situation created a beautiful contrast, an opportunity to see what communism can do and what capitalism can do. Not a single skyscraper had arisen on the communist part, not a single new building, not a single new road, no new factory – no creativity. Yes, they had distributed the wealth – they made the rich poor. And then the poor were not in a position to create wealth again.

Communism is based on a fallacious idea: the equality of man. Man is not equal.

The second idea is significant; but my interpretation of it is right, not what Marx said. The second idea says, "Equal opportunity for all." That's how it should be – equal opportunity for all, but remembering that everybody is unique, so everybody is going to use the equal opportunity to be very different from each other. The ultimate result is going to be individuals so different from each other that you cannot imagine it now.

According to Marx, equal opportunity means they will be all equal – equally wealthy, equally intelligent, equally healthy. That is sheer nonsense, because your parents were not my parents; you have different genes and different programs in your body. Now, there is no way to change the genes, the program – and small things make a difference.

So equal opportunity is a good idea and we should try it as far as humanly practical. But you should not be fanatic about it, because if you want perfect equality of opportunity then you are an idiot; that is not possible.

Just let me give you simple examples: if you are the eldest son in the family, then the youngest son in the family cannot have the same opportunity as the eldest, there is no way. Because you were the first to come, of course you received your mother and your father's love more because you were a novelty; then other children started coming and it was not anything new. The second boy was born, but he is going to be second. The eldest son in all the cultures is going to inherit the father's money. Why? It is not accidental: he got more love than anybody else, and he was the first to come.

Then the last son will also have a different status because he will be the smallest, favored by all, protected by all, all the brothers, the whole family. But the middle ones are nowhere, neither on this pole nor on that pole. They will not get the same attention as the first and the last. The last will become the favorite child of the family because now no more are coming; the last guest has come.

How can you give all equal opportunities? Either you will have to arrange births simultaneously so that a mother gives birth to twelve children simultaneously – equal opportunity.

But from the very beginning there is no equal opportunity. When a woman gets pregnant, neither she nor her husband are aware that there has been a car race; nobody is aware. When the sperms travel towards the egg it is just as in any race: they all stand in one line waiting for the third whistle, and then they run.

The mother's cell, the egg in the mother's womb, is waiting and the cells from the father's body, as they explode into the mother's body, start a great race – millions of sperms trying to reach the egg first. Whosoever reaches is the winner; all others will die. It is a question of life and death. It is no ordinary race in which you are defeated now and next time you get another chance. There is no next time – only a single opportunity for millions of alive cells. Only one makes it, because this is how it works. The mother's egg has a natural capacity so that once a male sperm has entered it, it closes. The others go on knocking around but within two hours they will all be dead.

There are losses all the way. And the way is not so small as you think, because for those small cells it is close to two miles, proportionately. If they were of your proportions then the passage would be two miles. And a great job they do, a marathon race! Of course, the strongest reaches.

They all start almost at the same time but from there, from the very impregnation, opportunities are different. Nobody knows those who have died, what kind of people they were. Somebody may have been an Albert Einstein, somebody a Ravi Shankar, somebody a Michelangelo. Nobody knows about those poor people who simply died in the first race and were not given any other chance.

And then small things in the life of the child... You cannot make them equal. For example, when Napoleon Bonaparte was six months old, his nurse, who was taking care of him, had just left him for a moment and a wild cat jumped onto Napoleon, put both his paws on his chest, and looked into his eyes. Immediately the nurse came back and chased the cat away, but Napoleon, for his whole life, remained afraid of cats. He was not afraid of lions, he could have wrestled bare-handed with a lion – there was no problem about it – but before a cat he simply became a nervous wreck.

Napoleon was defeated only once – his whole life was a life of victory. Just once he was defeated, by a British general who knew about his weakness. The general had gone with seventy cats ahead of him; seeing seventy cats, Napoleon lost all nerve, he forgot all about what to do and what not to do. It was not a victory by the general, it was a victory by the cats.

How can you manage to give equal opportunities to all? Now, if such a small incident can prove so fatal... Napoleon was a brave warrior before anybody, but nothing before a cat. The English general does not count at all, but he became victorious just by using a little psychology, just knowing about Napoleon s weakness – that when he saw a cat he could not think, he simply became frozen. And when Napoleon was in that nervous state, of course his whole army was at a loss; they had lost the man who was their life, their light and their guide.

Now, how can you manage equal opportunity for all children of the world? That's absolutely impossible. So don't try to take the communist idea to its logical end – then it becomes absurd.

Yes, with my interpretation – and my interpretation is that every-body should be given opportunities to be educated, opportunities to get food, opportunities to get clothes, opportunities to do anything that a person wants to do. There should be no discrimination about it;

opportunity should be given to everybody according to his talent and everybody according to his potentiality. But that is not happening in communism. In the name of equal opportunities everybody is forced to remain at the lowest denominator, because only there can you keep them equal. If you want them to be equal on a higher level, then you need more riches, more wealth – and that is missing. Equal opportunity can be made available, but what do you do with equal opportunity? You need people who can use these opportunities – and they don't need similar opportunities, they need different opportunities, equally different opportunities.

I am against communism because it is only a negative philosophy. I am all for commune-ism. That should be the right word: commune-ism.

A commune is respectful of every individual's uniqueness, repectful of every individual's talent, and tries to help his talent grow, help him grow towards his potential.

I want communes all over the world, so that slowly nations can disappear, and there are only communes: Living, small units of humanity, totally, joyously helping everybody to be himself.

Marx proposes the dictatorship of the proletariat, the dictatorship of the poor. That is stupid. They are poor, and if they are in power they will make everybody poor. What else can they do?

I propose a dictatorship of the enlightened ones. Nobody has proposed it up to now. And sometimes out of my crazy mind... This idea I have carried my whole life – dictatorship of the enlightened ones, because if it is of enlightened ones it cannot be dictatorship. It is a contradiction in terms. The enlightened person cannot be a dictator like Joseph Stalin or Adolf Hitler.

Yes, the enlightened person can dictate to you, but out of his love, not out of his power – he has no power – out of his insight, because he has eyes to see and to feel the potential of people.

His dictates can only be thought of as suggestions, advice, guidelines. Only in the dictatorship of the enlightened ones is there a possibility of a real, authentic democracy and also the real flowering of commune-ism: Equality by distributing riches, not poverty; destroying poverty from the very roots, and raising everybody upwards to be rich.

CHAPTER 6

Epilogue:
A Manifesto of One Humanity

The new man contains my whole philosophy about life and how it should be – lived in totality, in intensity, in wholeness, so that we are not only dragging ourselves from the cradle to the grave, but we can make each moment a tremendous rejoicing – a song, a dance, a celebration.

The old man that has existed up to now is on his death bed. He has suffered much; he needs all our compassion. He has been conditioned to live in misery, in suffering, in self-torture. He was given promises: promissory notes for great rewards after death – the more he suffers, the more he tortures himself, the more he is masochistic, the more he is destructive of his own dignity, the more he will be rewarded.

That was a very convenient concept for all the vested interests because the man who is ready to suffer can easily be enslaved. The man who is ready to sacrifice today for an unknown tomorrow has already declared his inclination to be enslaved. The future becomes his bondage. And for thousands of years, man has lived only in hope, in imagination, in dreams, in utopias, but not in reality. And there is no other life than the life of reality, than the life that exists in this moment.

The new man is a rebellion, a revolt, a revolution against all the conditionings which can enslave him, oppress him, exploit him, just by giving him hopes of a fictitious heaven, frightening him, blackmailing him about another fictitious phenomenon: hell. All the old ways of life were strangely in agreement on one point: that man is a sacrificial animal at the feet of a fictitious God.

There were times when men were actually sacrificed alive, butchered before stone statues. Although nobody dares to do such a thing now, psychologically the situation has not changed. Man is still sacrificed either in the name of communism, or in the name of capitalism, or in the name of an Aryan race, in the name of Islam, in the name of Christianity, in the name of Hinduism. Instead of stone gods, now there are only phony words, meaningless. But man has accepted to live like this for the simple reason that every child finds himself born in a crowd which is already conditioned. The teachers are conditioned, the parents are conditioned, the neighbors are conditioned; and the small child is almost helpless – he cannot envisage any other alternative than to be part of the crowd.

The old man was a crowd, a cog in the wheel; the old man had no individuality. The vested interests had taken all care to destroy self-respect, dignity, a joy and a gratefulness that you are a human being, that you are the highest creation in the long, long path of evolution…that you are the crowning glory.

These ideas were dangerous. If a man has some respect for himself, some dignity of being human, you cannot reduce him to a slave; you cannot destroy his soul and make him a robot. Up to now, man has only pretended to live – his life has been only hypothetical.

The new man is a revolt against the whole past.

He is a declaration that we are going to create a new way of life, new values of life; that we are destined for new goals – faraway stars are our targets. And we are not going to allow anybody to sacrifice us for any beautiful name. We are going to live our lives, not according to ideals, but according to our own longings, our own passionate intuitions. And we are going to live moment to moment; we are no longer to be befooled by the tomorrow, and the promises for tomorrow.

The new man contains the whole future of humanity. The old man is bound to die. He has prepared his own grave – he is digging it every moment, deeper and deeper. Nuclear weapons and all destructive measures are a preparation for a global suicide. The old man has decided to die. It is up to the intelligent people in the world to disconnect from the old man before he destroys you too…to disconnect yourself from old traditions, old religions, old nations, old ideologies.

For the first time, the old is no longer gold. The old is the rotten corpse of an ugly past. It is a great responsibility for the new generation, for the young people to renounce the past.

In the past, religions used to renounce the world. I teach you to love the world so that it can be saved, and to renounce the past totally and irrevocably, to be discontinuous.

The new man is not an improvement upon the old; he is not a continuous phenomenon, not a refinement. The new man is the declaration of the death of the old, and the birth of an absolutely fresh man – unconditioned, without any nation, without any religion, without any discriminations of men and women, of black and white, of East and West, or North and South.

The new man is a manifesto of one humanity. It is the greatest revolution the world has ever seen.

You have heard about the miracle that Moses parted the sea in two parts. That miracle is nothing. I want to part humanity, the whole ocean of humanity divided in two parts: the old and the new.

The new will love this life, this world. The new will learn the art of living and loving and dying. The new will not be concerned about heaven and hell, sin and virtue. The new man will be concerned about how to increase the joys of life, the pleasures of life – more flowers, more beauty, more humanity, more compassion. And we have the capacity and the potential to make this planet a paradise, and to make this moment the greatest ecstasy of your life.

Let the old die. Let the old be led by people like Ronald Reagan. Let the blind people follow the blind.

But those who have a younger spirit – and when I say "a younger spirit," it includes even those old people who are not old in spirit; and it does not include even the young people who are old in spirit. The spiritually young are going to be the new man.

The new man is not a hope: You are already pregnant with it.

My work is just to make you aware that the new man has already arrived. My work is to help you to recognize him and to respect him. You just have to drop all the dust that has gathered down the ages on the mirror of your consciousness.

The new man is not someone coming from another planet. The new man is you in your freshness, in your silences of the heart, in your depth of meditation, in your beautiful spaces of love, in your songs of joy, in your dances of ecstasy, in your love of this earth. No religion teaches you to love this earth – and this earth is your mother, and these trees are your brothers, and these stars are your friends.

In my vision you are already on the path of the new man. You have started the journey, although you are not fully awake; but as you will see the old man moving more and more towards the graveyard, it will become easier for you to renounce him and his ways of life, his churches, his synagogues, his temples, his gods, his holy scriptures.

Your holy scripture is your whole life, and nobody else can write it – you have to write it. You come with an empty book, and it depends on you what you make of it. Birth is not life; it is only an opportunity given to you to create life…to create a life as beautiful, as glorious, as loving as you can imagine, as you can dream.

The new man's dreams and his reality will be one because his dreams will be rooted here in this earth. They will bring flowers and fruits. They will not be just dreams – they will make the world a dreamland.

Realize the responsibility. Man has never faced a greater responsibility before: a responsibility to renounce the whole past, to erase it from your being.

Be Adam and Eve again, and let this earth be the Garden of Eden; and this time we will see who the God is who has the guts to drive man out of the Garden of Eden! It is going to be our garden, and if God wants to be in our garden, He will have to knock on our doors.

This earth can be a splendor, a magic, a miracle. Our hands have that touch – it is just that we have never tried it. Man has never given a chance to his own potential to grow, to blossom, to bring fulfillment, contentment, to shower the whole earth with flowers, to fill the whole earth with fragrance. To me, that fragrance is godliness.

The new man will not worship a God as a creator of the world; the new man will create God as a fragrance, as beauty, as love, as truth. Up to now God has been the creator: for the new man, man will be the creator, and God is going to be the created. We can create godliness – it is within our hands.

That's why I say the new man is the greatest revolution that has ever happened in the world. And there is no way to avoid it because the old man is determined to die, determined, committed to commit suicide. Let him die peacefully. Those who have a rebellious spirit should just disconnect themselves, and they will be the saviors, they will create a Noah's ark, they will be the beginning of a new world. And because we have known the old world and its miseries; we can avoid all those miseries; we can avoid all those jealousies, all those angers, all those wars, all those destructive tendencies....

We can go through a total transformation: we can create innocent people, loving people, people who breathe in freedom, people who help each other to be free. We can create nourishment for everybody to be dignified, to be respected – not according to some ideals and values, but just as he is.

The new man is going to be the very salt of the earth.

Can you say more about the qualities of a rebel? Is it the same thing as what you call the "new man"?

The qualities of a rebel are multidimensional. The first thing: the rebel does not believe in anything except his own experience. His truth is his only truth; no prophet, no messiah, no savior, no holy scripture, no ancient tradition can give him his truth. They can talk about truth, they can make much ado about truth, but to know about truth is not to know truth. The word "about" means around – to know about truth means to go around and around it. But by going around and around you never reach to the center.

The rebel has no belief system – theist or atheist, Hindu or Christian. He is an inquirer, a seeker. But a very subtle thing has to be understood: that is, the rebel is not an egoist. The egoist also does not want to belong to any church, to any ideology, to any belief system, but the reason for not belonging is totally different from that of the rebel. The egoist does not want to belong because he thinks too much of himself. He is too much of an egoist; he can only stand alone.

The rebel is not an egoist, he is utterly innocent. His nonbelieving is not an arrogant attitude but a humble approach. He is simply saying, "Unless I find my own truth, all borrowed truths are only burdening me, they are not going to unburden me. I can become knowledgeable, but I will not be knowing anything with my own being. I will not be an eyewitness of any experience." He does not belong to any church, any organization, because he wants not to be an imitator. He wants to remain pure and unpolluted so that he can search without any prejudice, so that he can remain open without any preconceived idea. But the whole approach is that of a humble person.

A rebel respects his own independence and also respects the independence of everybody else. He respects his own divineness and he respects the divineness of the whole universe. The whole universe is his temple – that's why he has left the small temples made by man. The whole universe is his holy scripture – that's why he has left all holy scriptures written by man. But it is not out of arrogance, it is out of a humble search. The rebel is as innocent as a child.

The second dimension will be not to live in the past, which is no more, and not to live in the future, which is not yet, but to live in the present with as much alertness and consciousness as one can manage. In other words, to live consciously in the moment. Ordinarily we live like somnambulists, sleepwalkers. The rebel tries to live a life of awareness. Awareness is his religion, awareness is his philosophy, awareness is his way of life.

The third dimension is that the rebel is not interested in domination over others. He has no lust for power, because that is the ugliest thing in the world. The lust for power has destroyed humanity and has not allowed it to be more creative, to be more beautiful, to be more healthy, to be more wholesome. And it is this lust for power that ultimately leads to conflicts, competitions, jealousies and finally to wars.

Lust for power is the foundation of all wars. If you look at human history…the whole of human history is nothing but a history of wars, man killing man. Reasons have changed, but the killing continues. It seems reasons are only excuses. The real fact is that man enjoys killing.

In one of Aesop's fables – and those are some of the greatest fables in the world, so simple and so significant – a small sheep is drinking water from a mountain stream of crystal-clear water. A great lion comes and naturally becomes interested in the sheep – it is breakfast time. But he has to find an excuse for his behavior, so he says to the sheep, "You are dirtying the stream. Don't you understand that I am the king of the jungle?"

The poor sheep says, "But your highness, I am standing below you so even if the water becomes dirty by my drinking, the water is going downstream – not towards you. You are making it dirty and I am drinking that dirty water. So your logic is not right."

The lion saw the point and became very angry. He said, "You don't have respect for your elders. You have some nerve arguing with me."

The poor sheep said, "I have not argued, I have simply said what was factual. You can see that the stream is going this way."

The lion was silent for a moment and then said, "Now I remember. You belong to a very uncultured, uneducated family. Your father insulted me yesterday."

The poor sheep said, "It must have been somebody else, because my father has been dead for three months, and you must know that he is within your belly. He is no longer alive because you have made a lunch of him. How can he behave disrespectfully toward you? He is dead!"

That was too much. The lion jumped and caught hold of the sheep saying, "You don't know manners, you don't know etiquette, you don't know how to behave."

The sheep said, "The simple fact is, it is breakfast time. Simply eat me; there is no need to find any excuse."

In such simple parables, Aesop has done miracles. He has said so much about man.

A rebel simply lives his life in the moment, with awareness, with no desire to dominate. He does not have any lust for power. He is a scientist of the soul – that is the fourth dimension. Just as science uses doubt, skepticism, inquiry, he uses the same methods for his inner search. Science uses them for objective reality, he uses them for his subjectivity. But he does not condemn doubt, he does not condemn skepticism, he does not condemn disobedience, he does not condemn a nonbelieving approach to reality. He enters within his own being with a scientific mind.

The rebel's religion is not superstitious, it is scientific. His religion is not a search for God, because to begin with God means you have already accepted a belief, and if you have accepted a belief your search is contaminated from the very beginning.

The rebel goes into his inner world with open eyes, with no idea of what he is looking for. He goes on polishing his intelligence. He goes on making his silences deeper, his meditation more profound, so that whatever is hidden in him is revealed to him; but he has no preconceived idea of what he is looking for.

He is basically an agnostic. That word has to be remembered because it describes one of his basic qualities. There are theists who believe in God, there are atheists who do not believe in God and there are agnostics who simply say, "We do not know yet. We will search, we will see. We cannot say anything before we have looked into every nook and cranny of our being." The rebel begins with, "I do not know." That's why I say he is just like a small child, innocent.

Two boys were discussing running away from home. "But if our fathers catch us they will hit us," said one.

"So," said the other, "we will hit them back."

"But we can't do that," said the first boy. "The Bible teaches us to honor our father and our mother."

"Right. Then you hit my father and I will hit yours."

Just an innocent and simple solution, with no difficulty.

The rebel lives a childlike innocence, and innocence is the most mysterious phenomenon. It opens the doors of all the secrets of life.

Only a rebellious person is truly revolutionary and is truly religious. He does not create an organization, he does not create a following, he does not create churches.

But it is possible that rebels can be fellow travelers: they may enjoy to be together, to dance together, to sing together, to cry and weep together, to feel the immensity of existence and the eternity of life together. They can merge into a kind of communion without any surrender of anybody's individuality; on the contrary, the communion of rebels refreshes everybody's individuality, nourishes everybody's individuality, gives dignity and respect to everybody's individuality.

About Osho

Osho defies categorization. His thousands of talks cover everything from the individual quest for meaning to the most urgent social and political issues facing society today. Osho's books are not written but are transcribed from audio and video recordings of his extemporaneous talks to international audiences. As he puts it, "So remember: whatever I am saying is not just for you... I am talking also for the future generations."

Osho has been described by *The Sunday Times* in London as one of the "1000 Makers of the 20th Century" and by American author Tom Robbins as "the most dangerous man since Jesus Christ." *Sunday Mid-Day* (India) has selected Osho as one of ten people – along with Gandhi, Nehru and Buddha – who have changed the destiny of India.

About his own work Osho has said that he is helping to create the conditions for the birth of a new kind of human being. He often characterizes this new human being as "Zorba the Buddha" – capable both of enjoying the earthy pleasures of a Zorba the Greek and the silent serenity of a Gautama the Buddha.

Running like a thread through all aspects of Osho's talks and meditations is a vision that encompasses both the timeless wisdom of all ages past and the highest potential of today's (and tomorrow's) science and technology.

Osho is known for his revolutionary contribution to the science of inner transformation, with an approach to meditation that acknowledges the accelerated pace of contemporary life. His unique OSHO Active Meditations™ are designed to first release the accumulated stresses of body and mind, so that it is then easier to take an experience of stillness and thought-free relaxation into daily life.

Two autobiographical works by the author are available:
Autobiography of a Spiritually Incorrect Mystic,
St Martins Press, New York (book and eBook)
Glimpses of a Golden Childhood,
OSHO Media International, Pune, India

OSHO International Meditation Resort

Location

Located 100 miles southeast of Mumbai in the thriving modern city of Pune, India, the OSHO International Meditation Resort is a holiday destination with a difference. The Meditation Resort is spread over 28 acres of spectacular gardens in a beautiful tree-lined residential area.

Uniqueness

Each year the Meditation Resort welcomes thousands of people from more than 100 countries. The unique campus provides an opportunity for a direct personal experience of a new way of living – with more awareness, relaxation, celebration and creativity. A great variety of around-the-clock and around-the-year program options are available. Doing nothing and just relaxing is one of them!

All programs are based on the OSHO vision of "Zorba the Buddha" – a qualitatively new kind of human being who is able *both* to participate creatively in everyday life *and* to relax into silence and meditation.

OSHO Meditations

A full daily schedule of meditations for every type of person includes methods that are active and passive, traditional and revolutionary, and in particular the OSHO Active Meditations™. The meditations take place in what must be the world's largest meditation hall, the OSHO Auditorium.

OSHO Multiversity

Individual sessions, courses and workshops cover everything from creative arts to holistic health, personal transformation, relationship and life transition, work-as-meditation, esoteric sciences, and the "Zen" approach to sports and recreation. The secret of the OSHO Multiversity's success lies in the fact that all its programs are combined with meditation, supporting the understanding that as human beings we are far more than the sum of our parts.

OSHO Basho Spa

The luxurious Basho Spa provides for leisurely open-air swimming surrounded by trees and tropical green. The uniquely styled, spacious Jacuzzi, the saunas, gym, tennis courts…all these are enhanced by their stunningly beautiful setting.

Cuisine

A variety of different eating areas serve delicious Western, Asian and Indian vegetarian food – most of it organically grown especially for the Meditation Resort. Breads and cakes are baked in the resort's own bakery.

Night life

There are many evening events to choose from – dancing being at the top of the list! Other activities include full-moon meditations beneath the stars, variety shows, music performances and meditations for daily life.

Or you can just enjoy meeting people at the Plaza Café, or walking in the nighttime serenity of the gardens of this fairytale environment.

Facilities

You can buy all your basic necessities and toiletries in the Galleria. The Multimedia Gallery sells a large range of OSHO media products. There is also a bank, a travel agency and a Cyber Café on-campus. For those who enjoy shopping, Pune provides all the options, ranging from traditional and ethnic Indian products to all of the global brand-name stores.

Accommodation

You can choose to stay in the elegant rooms of the OSHO Guesthouse, or for longer stays opt for one of the OSHO Living-In program packages. Additionally there is a plentiful variety of nearby hotels and serviced apartments.

www.osho.com/meditationresort
www.osho.com/guesthouse
www.osho.com/livingin

More Books and eBooks by OSHO Media International

The God Conspiracy:
The Path from Superstition to Super Consciousness

Discover the Buddha: 53 Meditations to Meet the Buddha Within
Gold Nuggets: Messages from Existence

OSHO Classics
The Book of Wisdom: The Heart of Tibetan Buddhism.
The Mustard Seed: The Revolutionary Teachings of Jesus
Ancient Music in the Pines: In Zen, Mind Suddenly Stops
The Empty Boat: Encounters with Nothingness
A Bird on the Wing: Zen Anecdotes for Everyday Life
The Path of Yoga: Discovering the Essence and Origin of Yoga
And the Flowers Showered: The Freudian Couch and Zen
Nirvana: The Last Nightmare: Learning to Trust in Life
The Goose Is Out: Zen in Action
Absolute Tao: Subtle Is the Way to Love, Happiness and Truth

The Tantra Experience: Evolution through Love
Tantric Transformation: When Love Meets Meditation

Pillars of Consciousness (illustrated)
BUDDHA: His Life and Teachings and Impact on Humanity
ZEN: Its History and Teachings and Impact on Humanity
TANTRA: The Way of Acceptance
TAO: The State and the Art

Authentic Living

Danger: Truth at Work: The Courage to Accept the Unknowable
The Magic of Self-Respect: Awakening to Your Own Awareness
Born With a Question Mark in Your Heart

OSHO eBooks and "OSHO-Singles"

Emotions: Freedom from Anger, Jealousy and Fear
Meditation: The First and Last Freedom
What Is Meditation?
The Book of Secrets: 112 Meditations to Discover the Mystery Within

20 Difficult Things to Accomplish in This World
Compassion, Love and Sex
Hypnosis in the Service of Meditation
Why Is Communication So Difficult, Particularly between Lovers?
Bringing Up Children
Why Should I Grieve Now?: facing a loss and letting it go
Love and Hate: just two sides of the same coin

Next Time You Feel Angry...
Next Time You Feel Lonely...
Next Time You Feel Suicidal...

OSHO Media BLOG
http://oshomedia.blog.osho.com

For More Information

www. **OSHO**.com

a comprehensive multi-language website including a magazine, OSHO Books, OSHO Talks in audio and video formats, the OSHO Library text archive in English and Hindi and extensive information about OSHO Meditations. You will also find the program schedule of the OSHO Multiversity and information about the OSHO International Meditation Resort.

http://OSHO.com/AllAboutOSHO
http://OSHO.com/Resort
http://OSHO.com/Shop
http://www.youtube.com/OSHO
http://www.Twitter.com/OSHO
http://www.facebook.com/pages/OSHO.International

To contact OSHO International Foundation:
www.osho.com/oshointernational,
oshointernational@oshointernational.com